SIMON SCOTT

Making a difference

Reflections of a children's social worker

mereo

Mereo Books

2nd Floor, 6-8 Dyer Street, Cirencester, Gloucestershire, GL7 2PF
An imprint of Memoirs Books. www.mereobooks.com
and www.memoirsbooks.co.uk

MAKING A DIFFERENCE

ISBN: 978-1-86151-843-9

First published in Great Britain in 2020
by Mereo Books, an imprint of Memoirs Books.

The address for Memoirs Books can be
found at www.mereobooks.com

Mereo Books Ltd. Reg. No. 12157152

Typeset in 11/15pt Century Schoolbook
by Wiltshire Associates.
Printed and bound in Great Britain

Contents

Foreword

It has taken a period of lockdown over the threat of the Covid 19 virus to persuade me finally to attempt what had crossed my mind several times since my retirement as a children and families social worker in 2019, after over forty years in this field – to record some of my experiences and reflect on my career.

I qualified in South Africa in 1975 and spent the next five years practising in that country before moving to England. Throughout, I worked in government or local authority settings until I became self-employed as an Independent Social Worker in 2006. My career has been steeped in statutory social work.

I have experienced many emotionally wrenching situations working with troubled families, and on some occasions I have struggled to persuade myself that my actions were in the best interests of the children concerned. In many instances though, thankfully, the decision has been straightforward. However drastic the action you are taking there have been many occasions when the evidence has pointed to that action being necessary to protect the children.

But drastic action most often brings pain to one or all members of the family. Whilst witnessing such pain, I have often found a need to comfort myself in the knowledge that the decisions are not taken by myself, but in consultation. In the case of drastic actions, too, it is often up to magistrates or a judge ultimately to decide whether the decision is right or not.

Much depends on the setting in which one is working. There are differences in the legislative framework between South Africa and England, of course. I will seek to explore, in broad outline, some that have affected my practice.

In addition, over the course of my career there have been changes in legislation following government reviews of the provision of services to children and families. The most sweeping change I experienced was the enactment of the Children Act 1989, which brought together the very many disparate pieces of legislation that had preceded it. Although there have since been several changes, the Act has provided a lasting framework.

Besides legislation, practice is heavily influenced by the resources available to assist us. Geography makes a difference: towns and cities in South Africa are much more widely distributed than in England, affecting the availability of local resources when one is working in the more remote areas.

Much social work can feel routine, but in many instances we are working to support a struggling family to ensure that the children can safely remain in the parents' care. Alternatively, it can be to support children who have had to be placed in care and to try to maximise their opportunities to manage in difficult circumstances.

So, the decision has finally been made to put my thoughts on paper. Names have been changed, of course. It would be remarkable, anyway, in such a long career for me to have remembered many of them.

The thoughts are my own. I have not sought to make this an academic book and I do not claim therefore that my musings are necessarily in line with current academic thinking or research. I have sought, rather, to give a general account of a long and varied career, whilst giving some explanations about the background and the thinking behind decisions I have taken.

Proceeds from the sale of the book will be donated to the Social Workers' Benevolent Trust, whose aim is to help social workers who find themselves in financial difficulties.

Chapter 1

Moving children

"Wanneer sal ons weer ons Ma sien?" A small voice from the back of the car. My Afrikaans was never good enough for lengthy conversations, but this I could well understand: "When will we see our Mum again?"

I am in a Government Garage-issued car – the GGs, as they were colloquially called because that was what appeared on the number plates – speeding along a South African road with no fewer than six children crowded into it, none of whom I had met before that morning.

I could hardly have expected something like this when I had decided to become a social worker. It was a unique experience for someone in his mid-twenties, and only a year or two into my career. Happily, I never again had to remove so many children from the care of their parents at one time. Nor would I have to do it on my own!

It was the only time too, bar one other occasion, that I had children in the car whom I had never met before. However, on that other occasion the children's mother was accompanying us on those long South African roads. But that is another story and one for a later chapter.

So, what led to a situation in which six children, ranging in age from fifteen to one or two, were in the charge of a stranger, being taken a couple of hundred miles from their home? It alarms me particularly that this was before the days of laws concerning wearing seatbelts for back seat passengers, and we would have been travelling at 50 or 60 miles per hour, at times along un-tarmacked roads. My recall is that we did not have a child seat either: the youngest was cradled in the arms of one of his teenage siblings. We had left mid-afternoon too, which meant we would arrive at our destination in the dark.

This was at a time when I was working a large area, stretching for some 200 miles, representing the Department of Social Welfare and Pensions. My caseload of around fifty or sixty cases therefore did not receive very frequent visits. Trips to the more remote areas, involving overnight stays, sometimes necessitated quick decisions and action.

On this trip, as always, my first port of call had been to the local magistrates' court to learn if there were matters awaiting my attention. I was advised that there was concern about a family in the next town on my journey. The family consisted of six children whose father had disappeared; he was sought by the Railway Police for alleged theft of railway property. The family had been joined by an "uncle", although it was suspected that he was not really the children's uncle.

There was general concern about the children's school attendance and home circumstances. I often had very little detail available to me but, of course, names and addresses were provided. I was spending the night in the town in which the court was situated, and I had time therefore to contact my office to check if any background information was available.

Later that day, my manager was able to inform me that the family had previously been on the books of one of the private welfare agencies in the Transvaal. The agency had been on the point of approaching the court to ask for removal of the children from the parents' care when the family disappeared.

It was therefore with this concerning information that I arrived at the address in the next town the following morning, one of many houses provided in the area for railway workers there. At home I found the oldest, a 15-year-old I will call Janie Smit, with his baby brother. Asked why he was not at school, he said he had stayed at home to look after his brother. I asked to be shown around the home.

This was a stark example of how practice then differed from how I would go about proceedings in England. Attitudes to authority in 1970s South Africa were very different. In England, I would never ask a child to show me around the home without an adult's permission: I simply would not have the authority to do so. Another issue is that talking to a child without an adult present in such a situation as this would now be considered a serious breach of the family's privacy and I would be laying myself open to charges of unprofessional practice.

In South Africa I gave no thought to such issues, and the fact that I asked Janie to show me around was never questioned. I found the kitchen to be clean enough, but there were only meagre amounts of food for a large family.

Sleeping facilities consisted of mattresses on the floor, covered by old candlewick bedspreads and therefore showing little evidence of warmth or comfort. The only double mattress indicated that mother and "uncle" were sharing.

I had obviously asked Janie where his mother was and had been told that she was visiting a friend with one of the other younger children. By this stage it was clear to me that I would need some persuasion that there was any alternative to taking the children into care. The situation could not wait another month before my next visit, and in any case the history suggested that there was a risk that the family would again disappear.

My office had told me that they would be putting together contingency plans for the accommodation of the children, as the information then available had suggested that this might turn out to be necessary.

I asked Janie to take me to his mother. I seem to recall that I had only a short interview with Mrs Smit, which served only to confirm the information that I already had. Mr Smit's whereabouts were unknown (or, at least, as far as she was prepared to admit) and she was struggling to hold together the care of six children. Evidently for a start, she was unable to ensure that Janie attended school regularly.

I remember announcing – I cannot really use any other term – that I had decided I would be taking the children into care. I am not sure why there was no significant resistance: just many questions about what the future might hold, such as where the children would be, how soon they could be seen, and the legal process that would inevitably follow. Perhaps Mrs Smit was too defeated by her family situation to argue against my decision.

In South Africa at the time, social workers had the legal power to make decisions about the immediate removal of children from the parents' care. This case provides a good illustration of why such a power existed, with many families located a great distance from a court where there was a magistrate who could make such decisions. These magistrates were specialists in children's legislation and were termed Commissioners of Child Welfare. Any decision by a social worker to remove children had to be brought before a Commissioner within 72 hours for ratification.

I asked Mrs Smit to accompany me to get the other children out of school. We all returned to the family home to collect what belongings the children could pack before I headed off with the children: four in the back seat and two in the front.

How I cringe now at the thought! And how devastated and scared the children must have felt. Their only consolation was that they were together and able to support each other, and for this I was very thankful indeed. As I have said, my Afrikaans was not up to the standard of maintaining long conversations, and I was grateful that the younger children, probably from habit, tended to direct their questions at their older siblings. At least I was able to understand the conversations and intervene if necessary.

As happens in many large families, the older children can take on a caring and protective role beyond their years. I quickly gained the impression that the oldest two regularly took on such a role. Of course, the fact that Janie was happy to care for his young sibling rather than go to school suggested that he was well used to acting as a surrogate parent.

So how does one answer the question, "When will we see our mother again?" Throughout my career, I have held that children are more able to manage being told painful truths than we sometimes give them credit for. I have maintained that this is preferable to fibs or half-truths that can be hurtful and damaging later, when they turn out to be untrue. I have been conscious, though, that some colleagues, foster parents and others have preferred to cushion children from harsher realities. I am unsure which is the best way. Of course, I always tried to be as sensitive as I could in the way I disclosed painful truths to children.

On this point, my career spans a time when it was thought best not to disclose to babies who were adopted that they were not being brought up by their birth parents. It was thought that believing they were born into the family would give them a greater sense of security.

I have been involved with teenagers who have gone right off the rails when they have learned that they had been brought up with this lie. Their whole world of security can feel to them to have been destroyed. Thank goodness thinking has moved on, and children are now usually given a Life Story Book that adoptive parents can share with the child, explaining the circumstances around their adoption in the kindest way possible, thus preventing a huge shock in finding out the truth later in life.

More often these days, I have come across several situations in which parents will not tell children that their stepfather, or their mother's partner, is not their natural father. When I have presented arguments about the difficulties that can arise later, these parents have usually told me that they are waiting for the right time. The problem is determining what is the right time. The fact is that younger children can handle such things much better than older children. Growing up with the knowledge is better than finding out, sometimes by some random event or conversation, when the child can feel betrayed.

While I am on this subject, I will digress a little further. I once placed a baby, Elizabeth, for adoption and provided the adoptive parents with a Life Story book. The adoptive mother told me that her husband was very much against the use of such a book, again feeling that it would be difficult for Elizabeth to be faced with painful realities at a young age. A few weeks later, though, the adoptive mother told me that her husband, once he had read the book, had immediately started introducing it to Elizabeth. Such books seek to present the birth parents in as positive a light as possible and to try to prevent the child feeling rejected by them, whilst also being truthful about how they ended up being "specially chosen" by their adoptive parents.

I had the pleasure of meeting Elizabeth after she had turned sixteen. I was contacted by a social worker saying that she wanted to meet her birth mother. She would have the right to do so after she turned eighteen, but in the meantime she wanted to meet me.

Of course, I agreed: I was intrigued! Accompanied by her social worker, Elizabeth asked me about my work with her and her parents so many years previously. I recall her words clearly: "I love my parents, but it is like I have a hole in my tummy and I just want to meet my birth mum". The adoptive parents had accepted Elizabeth's wishes in this regard.

She had been warned of the risk of either not being able to trace her birth mother, or indeed her birth mother refusing to meet her. I reinforced this message and suggested that if she waited until after she turned eighteen, she might be more able to manage such difficulties. Nevertheless, I happily gave her a short tour, stopping outside the hospital where she was born and showing her the birth parents' home at the time of her birth. She was very busy clicking away with her camera.

How does Fate work? What are the odds against Elizabeth's birth mother still living in the same home some fifteen years after she had Elizabeth in her care and, during the twenty seconds or so that we were stopped outside the home for a photograph, that she should be seen walking back home along the pavement? They must be huge, but it happened, and Elizabeth cried "There she is!" She had recognised her from a photograph in her Life Story book.

I drove away hastily: it would be highly inauspicious for them to meet without preparation and the birth mother being forewarned. I heard a while later that the social worker had eventually decided to make an approach to the birth mother by letter. She had responded positively, and Elizabeth had been enabled to meet her.

* * *

Back to the six anxious Smit children. When would they next see their mother? The truth was that I did not know and as far as I can remember, I could only give a non-committal response, but I added that we would be doing as much as we could to ensure that it happened.

Their mother had naturally been distressed at the removal of the children, but had handled the situation well. She, of course, had details of how to contact me and information about the fact that the matter would go before the Commissioner of Child Welfare in my office's town. I had only met her a few hours before and could only hope that she would soon be in touch and able to visit the children.

In my long career I have been involved, sadly, in the removal of several children from their parents' care. This can vary from parents who are requesting that the child or children are received into care for a short time during a period when respite care is necessary because of varied circumstances, to traumatic removal from highly resistant parents, with police assisting in the process.

The manner in which the parents manage the process has a huge impact, for obvious reasons, on how well the children can cope with it. Children can accept, however reluctantly, a traumatic separation more easily if their parents can provide reassurance and support. Mrs Smit had admirably answered the children's questions as best she could but inevitably, there remained many unanswered questions about their future.

By the time our journey was over, darkness had fallen and the younger ones were asleep. Our first port of call was the home of some foster parents who had undertaken to care for the baby. Looking back, this was my only contact with any foster parents during the five years I was in practice in South Africa. My agency, the Department of Social Welfare and Pensions, dealt mainly with teenagers, whilst younger children were the remit of a private charity, the Child Welfare Society. Janie and his teenage sister provided as many answers to the foster parents as they could regarding the baby's routine and again, they handled this remarkably well despite their reluctance to part with him.

Thereafter, we had a short journey to the Place of Safety. At the time, children received into care would be placed in this government-run children's home until decisions were made regarding their future care. The advantage of this situation was that five children were being placed together, and this would have been an immense source of comfort for them.

At the time, it was a pragmatic decision to separate the older children from the youngest, as the Place of Safety was not designed or equipped to take on babies. Nowadays, for obvious reasons, it is considered good practice to keep siblings together as much as possible. Sibling relationships can remain an important source of support and belonging well into adulthood.

Except in an emergency, any decision to separate children would be taken only after careful analysis of balance of harm. An important consideration would be how contact between the siblings could be facilitated.

I have been involved in a few cases of this. Sometimes children have been so affected by their experiences before coming into care, or even whilst in care, that their behaviour towards each other is considered more destructive than helpful. For instance, receiving individual attention from the carers without jealous reactions from a sibling can be beneficial to both children. Unfortunately, on some occasions, siblings have to be separated simply because there is no placement that would be able to have them all together.

I have limited recall of what happened to the Smit family after I had placed them. The case was taken on by a worker who had responsibility within the town in which our office was located. What I do recall is that

Mr Smit reappeared remarkably quickly, suggesting that he was in communication with his wife throughout their separation. Mr and Mrs Smit moved into the town and were therefore able to visit the children.

I do know that Janie and one or two of the older siblings were placed by the court in a School of Industries. As I have said, I had no contact with foster carers other than my brief encounter placing the youngest of the Smit family. Foster carers were few and far between and used exclusively for young children. A standard way of placing older children was to make use of Schools of Industry. Although I was to see a few of my clients placed in these institutions, I never saw any of them, probably mainly because there were none that were less than a couple of hundred miles away. There were no alternatives at the time, but how difficult it must have been for these children, moved so far away from their parents.

I did learn that the younger children were, in time, returned to the care of their parents.

One of the features of being a social worker is that very often, one loses track of what happens to the children with whom one has been involved. I have frequently wished I knew how things had turned out in the long run. Social work so often involves making the best decision one can, based on the evidence at the time. Inevitably it is not an exact science and at times I wondered whether the decision made was the right one in the long run for the children concerned.

I do believe that the little information I gleaned about the outcome for the Smit family indicates that the right decision was made for the children. They were living in very sparse circumstances, with an "uncle" I never did meet and a mother who was having to cope with knowing her husband's whereabouts but having to keep this from the police. I have little doubt that at least the older children were also having to keep this secret. The parents' coping skills had also been in doubt for some years.

Much would depend, I suppose, on the regime in the Schools of Industry. Press reports and investigations that I am aware of suggest that children have been mistreated and abused in some large institutions in many countries. I saw no research on the outcomes of these institutions in South Africa.

Here in England, there would have been many resources available that could have been plugged in to the family in the hope that this could avert the necessity of removing the children. In the circumstances, the drastic action taken seems to have stabilised the family's situation for the children's benefit and, I hope, given them a better chance of reaching their potential. That, after all, must be one of the primary aims of social work with children and families.

Chapter 2

The beginnings

I did not follow a conventional path into social work. It could almost be said that I landed in it by default.

I believe that most of my colleagues here in England would have undertaken some form of work within the general sphere of social services provision before moving on to seeking qualification as a social worker. In South Africa when I entered university most of the students had progressed directly from school to reading for the social work degree. This specific degree was already a requirement for qualification as a social worker.

Having spent six years in banking after leaving school, I was the oldest student on the course and was considered to be a "mature student". I had grown tired of work in a bank, which can become rather repetitive, and I was also disillusioned with a business where it can seem that money is the be-all and end-all of life.

This led to a decision in 1972 to read for a degree. The university ran an advisory service and through this I was given an aptitude test. The result was a recommendation that I should pursue a career involving figures! I had just opted out of banking, so that choice was a non-starter. Somehow, the second option that appeared was to become a librarian. I really am unsure where that came from: reading had never been high on my list of priorities in my early years. Beano and Eagle comics were my particular favourites. I recall with some embarrassment that I wrote my matriculation exam having read one of my set works in the Classics Illustrated version only. Oh dear!

The third suggestion from the aptitude test was that I work with people. Aha!

Having decided on this third option, the logical course was a Social Science degree. I recall sitting in a large hall full of youngsters (mainly) who had made a similar decision in order to hear guidance on choices available, when a lady with large glasses and a big smile came onto the stage to try to persuade us to opt for social work. I even recall her name, as she was one of the social work lecturers, Cecile Rosenthal. Sadly, no longer with us.

I have always found making decisions difficult, particularly when there are several options available. I guess I follow a classic male trait by buying the first thing that comes available when shopping, rather than exploring lots of shops to compare other options. Interesting, then, that I landed in a career that involves a lot of decision-making that can often affect the whole of a child's future. However, besides quite liking the sound of working with people to try to improve their lives, or perhaps to attempt to ensure their safety and well-being, I was attracted by the fact that the social work degree was pretty well mapped out, with little by way of choice of subjects if you wanted to achieve qualification.

It was a three-year course, with a requirement unsurprisingly to undertake the social work course for all of the three years. A further requirement was that the student undertook three years of either Sociology or Psychology, and two years in the other. I opted in the end for three years of Sociology and two in Psychology. For a reason I cannot recall, part of the Psychology course involved the dissection of a rat. That was a strong motivator for me to prefer the Sociology alternative, particularly having been a vegetarian since my marriage!

Thus, I had little by way of decision-making, as these requirements left only two further courses to choose in the first two years and, for me, it was an easy decision to choose music.

Having therefore "gone in blind" so to speak, tumbling into a career in social work, the fact that I pursued that career for just over forty years is proof enough, I believe, that I had made the right decision for myself.

It was during the third year of study that I was introduced to carrying responsibility for a live case. And perhaps inevitably, in South Africa during the years of Apartheid, I was thrown into racial issues. Such issues confront social workers in most countries of the world, I would have thought, but the South African system brought it into sharp relief.

The Apartheid system of classification of all citizens into the four categories of White, Indian, Coloured (mixed race) and Black was strictly enforced. Several of our lecturers were highly conscious of the activities of the Bureau of State Security (BOSS), which was widely believed, with good cause, to have its tentacles everywhere and to have many "informers", particularly in universities. Any anti-state ideas were carefully policed, but a primary focus was ideas that smacked of communism, with anyone believed to be a communist likely to face arrest, deportation, or even quiet disappearance. This made the teaching of Sociology particularly difficult. I remember lecturers were careful to stress that the subject matter of their lectures was theories, and not their own ideas or beliefs.

My first case, then, was a swift introduction into a world way outside my previous experience, having been brought up in the middle-class White family of an Anglican priest.

I had already had a rude awakening from this, having at the age of 17 been required to undergo nine months of army training. That was not an adjustment to racial issues that I encountered in my first case, as the army training was an all-White affair, but a rude awakening nevertheless from a quiet life in a Rectory. I was to join a noisy train full of teenagers of various backgrounds, and I heard the use of more colourful language during that train trip than I had in all of my life thus far. I was resolved to avoid the use of such bad language. That resolution lasted only a day or two once corporals started ordering us around to do everything "at the double"!

The racial issues I refer to came in the form of a requirement to visit a local Coloured township, where there were concerns for some children whose father was said regularly to abuse alcohol. Sadly, this was not uncommon amongst the Coloured folk at the time, as I had learned from press reports and from my father during his work in a Coloured church.

(I should mention that the Anglican church, and indeed the major churches, other than the Afrikaans Dutch Reformed Church, refused to comply with the government's requirement that all institutions observe Apartheid principles. My father had emigrated from England to South Africa with a sense that he was called to work with minority populations and much of his career there focused on working with the Coloured people. Despite the churches' refusal to comply with Apartheid, people tended to orient within the churches to their own race group and sit separately. My father's church was attended virtually entirely by people classified as Coloured. Some years later my brother was a priest and had a mixed congregation in his church, but the races tended to sit separately despite being encouraged not to do so.)

I was given to understand that the Cape Coloureds, who were primarily Afrikaans speakers, had a sense of identity, although I was never to work with them or encounter them much. The Coloureds in my area however, an English-speaking group, did not have that sense of identity, unlike Whites, Indians and Blacks. Alcohol abuse was fairly prevalent, and so was domestic abuse. To make matters more complicated, the parents I was dealing with were a Coloured man and a Black woman. Housed in a Coloured area, the children were English-speaking and attended local Coloured schools, but their mother had a different identity and background, and hailed from a Zulu-speaking rural community.

What could a young, inexperienced social worker do in such a situation? It is so long since all this happened that I have limited recall of what I did. I do remember visiting and interviewing the mother a few times. I do not recall seeing the children or speaking to them much, nor indeed to their father. I was of course supervised by a lecturer, and had regular discussions with him about what I had learned from my visits.

In the end, the matter was returned to the agency that had responsibility for the case and I was told that the children were subsequently taken into care and their mother returned to her rural village.

Later, after qualifying, I had a memorable role in a case involving a similar racial set-up. When I started working, although there was a drive to have social workers from different government departments involved with their own racial groups, the Department of Coloured Affairs did not have sufficient social workers of that race, so for the first couple of years of my employment I had some involvement with Coloured cases.

This raised issues of cultural difference. I was once accused by my young clients in England of being "too posh" to understand them. The cultural differences between my upbringing and the lives of my Coloured clients were, by comparison, far starker.

I remember making one visit to a family with numerous children, all living in what amounted to one large corrugated iron room. Sheer curiosity led me to ask the parents, apologetically and despite it having nothing to do with the matter for which I was visiting, if they minded telling me how they managed to make love without the children being aware. They responded by saying they waited for the children to be asleep, which seemed to be rather ineffective given the crowded circumstances. I suppose there are very many children in the world who grow up with greater knowledge of sexual issues than I did, having been brought up in a home with several bedrooms.

Social work training emphasises the need to be aware of cultural issues and not to impose one's own views on families of a different background.

Part of our role was to visit the parents of children about to leave care, as they were near to finishing their schooling. Again, large distances could be involved, with children in institutions far from their relatives. Our role was limited to making a visit to parents and reporting back as to the likelihood of the child being returned to their care.

The situation I particularly recall was again a Coloured child born to a Zulu mother. I do not think the whereabouts, or perhaps even the identity, of the father was known. The addresses of Black people within their townships were almost invariably simply "care of" the local store. These stores – general shops selling a wide range of merchandise – were often owned and run by Indian people. (The Indian community in South Africa had arisen as a result of the recruitment in times past of people from India as labourers for the farming industry).

These store owners and workers knew everyone in the community. On this particular visit I was told that the woman I wanted to see lived on a far hill, which could not be accessed by road. I was offered the use of a horse and a Zulu guide, and it was by this means that I arrived, dressed in reasonably smart clothes and a tie, in the very dark home of my client. This was a typical round mud hut – a rondavel – which had a small fire burning in the middle. The rondavel did not have a window and I could only dimly make out the woman concerned sitting on the floor.

I was able to use my guide as a translator. I established, in what amounted to a very short interview indeed, that mother and daughter were long estranged. The mother spoke only Zulu, whilst the daughter, brought up in a Coloured institution, would be English-speaking and would be highly unlikely to know any Zulu at all.

Needless to say, my short report on my return made it clear that there would be no chance of her daughter returning to the care of her mother. I was told that the likely outcome would be that the daughter would move on to another institution for older children until she was able to become independent. How very sad.

These two cases illustrate one of the many negative effects of the Apartheid regime. The designation of areas by race could not accommodate the inevitable mixes between the races, and the divisions created were exacerbated by the different languages used within those areas. In this second case, an institutionalised Coloured child would have had an education of sorts, whilst her mother would have had little if any education. The effect was to drive what was presumably a lifelong wedge between parent and child. Sadly, the strict separation of racial groups meant that this was just seen as an unfortunate consequence of the system.

Looking back, there were so many aspects of the Apartheid system that I and my family railed about, but ultimately we did not become politically active in seeking to effect changes. We were not alone. We Whites were able to use our votes at elections, but the Nationalist Party always predominated. I mentioned the extensive security network that I was particularly aware of during my university training. This made active opposition to the system highly likely to lead to close monitoring, swift incarceration, or in some cases deportation.

The mantra of Apartheid was separate but equal development. The reality was completely different. One area in which this was blatantly portrayed was regarding salaries paid to government employees. These were calculated on the basis of 1:2:2:4 – salaries for White employees amounted to double those paid to Coloured and Indian staff, and four times the pay of Black workers. I recall that the private social work agencies struggled to raise funds to pay their staff equal salaries, despite the government subsidising social work salaries based on this highly discriminatory formula.

* * *

During my time in the Department of Social Welfare and

Pensions, we did have some limited involvement with adults, specifically those addicted to drugs and alcohol. The potential undermining effects of drugs was viewed by the government as a significant threat. It is perhaps unsurprising that a right-wing government such as existed then had what would by many be seen as rather draconian measures available for the treatment of addicts.

Anyone concerned about a person's addiction could apply to the court for assessment and possible treatment. There was little treatment available within the community and generally all such limited options had been tried by the time such a statutory assessment was applied for.

If the court determined, after assessment, that the person concerned was addicted, it could order their detention in a treatment facility for a period – three or six months, as far as I can recall. As with Schools of Industry, these facilities were many miles away. They were located in remote areas, enabling easier control of access to drugs and alcohol. It was the only measure in existence, I was told, where an adult could be detained against his will without having committed a crime.

I had no real knowledge of, and little training in, the problem of addiction. Was I really qualified therefore to make these assessments? I can say, though, that the cases I dealt with had such a long history of addiction that assessment was relatively straightforward. In any case, the court did not rely solely on the social work assessment but also on the evidence of whoever referred the person to the court.

One remarkably interesting episode I was involved in was a large exercise carried out by social workers and the police. The Department was closed for a couple of days, apart from emergencies, and we social workers accompanied the police to search local spots popular amongst homeless adults.

The aim was to carry out a survey of these "vagrants", as they were then termed. The police located them and stood by whilst we interviewed them to obtain information about their backgrounds. It made for an interesting diversion from our normal work.

What made it particularly interesting was that part of our remit was to offer treatment for drug or alcohol addiction. Six men accepted this and we interviewed them further at the office on the following day. It was then a matter of getting the court order, which was a formality in the circumstances. Our Department later received a letter from the treatment facility thanking us for sending this group there. The men, who knew each other, formed a motivated team which was a positive influence on others receiving treatment at the time. The facility was unused to receiving what were, in effect, voluntary patients and they greatly enjoyed working with them.

I will end this chapter by mentioning an issue that arose during my time in the Department and has occasionally given me thought since, that of dress code. I had a wonderful set of colleagues and diversity of personality and outlook was evident.

One social worker did not fit easily into the regime. He was committed and kind-hearted, but his views were rather anti-establishment – he argued with me once about whether it was right to make a child go to school, as the education he would be getting was of little worth in equipping him for life. I would not necessarily say he was wrong but holding a stance such as this when working within a department of a traditional, right-wing government did not sit right.

He strongly resisted wearing a tie and when management eventually made it clear that this was required, as he was "representing the Department", he conformed but wore it loosely over a shirt that did not have the top button done up! He made his point I guess, and management did not pursue the matter further.

In England, there is far more informality and no firm requirements, to my knowledge. The only time I came across management insistence was a member of staff being asked not to wear a CND badge, as the profession should not be reflecting an activist stance whilst at work.

There is a body of opinion that dressing formally emphasises difference when visiting disadvantaged families. Rather, when trying to form relationships with clients and getting alongside them, more informal dress would perhaps be helpful.

I have always chosen to wear a tie. I believe that this reflected my professional status and the reality of the situation. I have never been aware of it being a problem, although maybe it added to the view of the young people I mentioned who referred to me being "too posh" for them!

During the latter years of my career my work was exclusively involved with the courts. During that time, I often thought that some women social workers have looked far more informally dressed than men when attending court. The men have always come in suits and perhaps it is easier for us, because this an expectation of professionals. Women have more choices and at times I have wondered how some social workers' dress has reflected on their professional status. One solicitor whispered to me at court that the social worker looked like she was dressed in her pyjamas!

No doubt there are many differing opinions on this tricky subject.

Chapter 3

Child sexual abuse

I mentioned in my opening chapter that there was another memorable occasion that saw me whizzing children I had known for only a few hours towards my home base.

Social work is founded on the idea of building relationships with your clients in order to use your influence to improve the family's functioning. Emphasis is placed on making relationships with the children with whom you are dealing and to give them a voice in what happens to them.

As we have seen, that ability is severely limited when the location of your office is remote; the frequency of visits is curtailed. Another factor is high caseloads. In England, I often had some difficulty with managing all that I was required to do with caseloads of 20 or 30 families, let alone the 60-odd cases I had when I first started out in South Africa.

One factor I noticed in working in small villages was the difficulty in maintaining confidentiality. In a Coloured township I visited, I was asked by a family what progress I was making with another family in the area. Our Government Garage cars – "The GGs are coming" – enabled the village to know the social worker was visiting and with which families they were involved.

Within a couple of years of my starting work, the Department of Coloured Affairs was able to assume responsibility for work with their race and we continued to work only with the White population. It was on one of my visits to a remote town that I again visited the local magistrate's office to see if there were any issues awaiting my attention. Very often there weren't, and I went about my other planned visits. On this occasion, though, I was told that a doctor had asked me to visit a woman who was one of his patients. She had approached him because she had an orange lodged in her vagina, which she and her husband were unable to extract. Now, please do not believe that this is a common request made to social workers. It is perhaps unsurprising that I have heard of no similar referral in my long career! The doctor had apparently had a fruitful session with Mrs Thomson in performing the extraction, but she wanted a visit from me.

I duly visited her with some trepidation, very curious, but also apprehensive as to what she would be asking of me. What in heaven's name could a young, male social worker, who visited the area about once a month, be asked to do in such a situation?

Mrs Thomson was a well-spoken woman, in a well-ordered, comfortable home. She was a little embarrassed, but she seemed reasonably at ease talking to me despite our age and gender difference, presumably because of my professional status. She explained that she had been married for about 15 years, but she felt unwilling to continue to try to meet her husband's excessive sexual demands. The frequency of these demands certainly sounded excessive to me! Mrs Thomson explained that attempts to bring some variation into sexual relations had developed into her husband inserting various fruits into his long-suffering wife, but the use of an orange had been a step too far and had led to the necessity of the trip to her doctor.

Although clear that she wanted to end the relationship forthwith, she felt unable to confront her husband about this and in any case lacked the means to move out with the children. She also believed it would be unsafe for them to move within the small town in which they lived. She wanted to be far away.

After consultation with my office, I was able to tell Mrs Thomson that a flat could be offered to her and the children on a temporary basis. She jumped at the opportunity. She set about packing clothes for herself and her two teenage children. She wrote a note for her husband to find on his return from work outlining her decision and providing my contact details. We then drove to the school and I left her to explain her plans to the head teacher and to take the children out of school there and then.

I do not recall any of our conversation on the long journey to the flat. What a huge shock this all must have been to the children! I think I would be able to remember if there had been much by way of protest from them, though. Obviously, the shock would have been greatly alleviated through knowing that they would be remaining in their mother's care, even if the longer-term future was uncertain.

It was early evening by the time we reached the flat, and I returned home. It was with great trepidation, though, that I went to work the next day. I had no idea how Mr Thomson would have taken the news he received through his wife's note, but I could imagine that he would be none too pleased. I tried to brace myself to face an irate telephone call from him. I prepared to argue that his wife was free to make her own decisions, but I would not be prepared to relinquish the care of the children to him without court proceedings in order to ensure their safety and well-being.

When the call came, however, a meek and pleading voice opened the conversation with, "Please, sir, can I have my family back?" I only had to say that I had been asked by his wife to keep their whereabouts from him, and we would need to discuss the future. He immediately agreed to travel to my office to see me the next day.

The outcome was swift, and far easier than I imagined. Mr Thomson visited as requested and agreed to be seen by a psychiatrist. A psychiatrist we contacted in the town happened to have a cancellation that day and saw him there and then. Mr Thomson accepted that he had an excessive sex drive and agreed to take medication for the problem.

Mrs Thomson was willing to meet him to reassure herself that he was agreeing to maintain his medication. She clearly gained this reassurance, as she agreed to return to the family home with him, together with the children.

A happy ending? I do not know – as so often happens in social work, one is left wondering how things turned out. However, looking back at this from several years of experience later, I am amazed at how I handled this.

Firstly, and importantly, this was at a time when the sexual abuse of children was either unknown, or never talked about. I recall nothing on this subject during my training. It simply did not cross my mind that the children might be involved in any way. I wonder now, though, how that sort of thing could be going on in the house for several years without the children at least being aware of it, and perhaps highly conscious of it as teenagers.

Secondly, the requirement these days of seeing the children and giving them a voice, again was not part of practice back then.

Perhaps I am being a bit hard on myself; after all, there was no indication that the children were in any way involved and I really therefore did not have a legal right to try to see them separately. Their parents had responsibility for the children's safety unless there was reason to believe they were not fulfilling this role adequately. However, there was no follow up, which is what I now believe I should have arranged.

To be fair, it would be at least another decade before the issue of child sexual abuse would be brought out into the open. Even then it took some time to gain further understanding of this problem, as well as for its prevalence to be accepted. Procedures and systems could then be implemented that aimed to address the issue.

I have sadly been involved in several cases of child sexual abuse and in fact at one stage I specialised in the assessment of alleged perpetrators. The vast majority of such assessments were undertaken by the Probation Service, dealing with offenders who were up before the courts for their offences. However, Social Services would on occasion be confronted with a dilemma over possible risk to children where a man (I was involved with only one female perpetrator) had joined the family and had had an allegation or allegations of child sexual abuse in the past that had not led to conviction.

If the man concerned had a conviction for such an offence, or indeed almost any offence against a child, the level of risk would be deemed high enough to take steps to protect the children involved. Cases where there were unproven allegations posed more difficulties. The Probation Service would not be involved, and I could be called upon to give an opinion regarding risk to the children concerned. Risk could usually be assumed: seldom are allegations made that can be summarily dismissed. The level of risk, however, would need to be assessed in each individual case.

One dramatic situation I faced was when I was carrying out an assessment with such an alleged offender. One thing is certain when allegations of child sexual abuse occur: there are inevitably huge family ructions that result. Mr Russet was no exception. His wish to join a family where there were children present caused alarm in the wider family. He had been suspected of abusing a child in the past and, although his new girlfriend was willing to believe he posed no risk to her children, her relations were not so trusting.

I always carried out these interviews jointly with another social worker. Mr Russet arrived for one interview with a large plastic bag, which he placed under the table between us and him. Soon after the interview started, he asked us to turn off the video recorder, but I always insisted on recording such assessment interviews in order to review the person's reactions and responses to questions.

We argued against turning the recorder off for some time, but Mr Russet kept insisting that he had something important to say but would not have it on video. In the end we had to balance up the loss of recorded evidence of what he had to say against the possibility that he would reveal significant information to inform the risk assessment if we stopped recording. In any case, anything said in front of two social workers would carry quite considerable weight evidentially. After all, most social work interviews are carried out alone, and therefore most statements that might be later disputed amount to the social worker's word against that of the person being interviewed. The word of two social workers would be more difficult for the client to counter.

We reluctantly agreed to switch off the recording, but what transpired was completely unexpected. Mr Russet revealed the contents of his package. It was an axe, which he almost reverentially placed on the table between us!

We immediately made it clear that we were not prepared to continue the interview in these circumstances, but Mr Russet hastily assured us that he meant no harm to us. All he wished to say was that he had purchased the axe that day, and that it was his intention to use it on a grandparent of the family he wished to join, who was opposing this.

He said this with no vehemence. He presented it as a firm but gentle statement of fact. What should we have done? The obvious answer is that we should have terminated the interview there and then and informed the police. We did not do that though. Perhaps it was because, from our previous knowledge of Mr Russet, it would be out of character for him to make such a dramatic move. Perhaps it was a result of our wish to pursue his thinking more and to understand it better.

We did insist that we would not proceed with the axe remaining where it was, and continuation of the planned interview would require that the recording be restarted.

Mr Russet was content to agree to both demands and we returned to interviewing him after removing the axe to a place well out of his reach. Later, we were able to inform the police and I was asked to make a statement at the police station. The fact that there was no follow up indicated perhaps that the police were able to confiscate the axe and to decide not to prosecute.

Ultimately, we were able to assess risk, both to ourselves and more importantly to the children. Again, it seems obvious that we should have concluded this without proceeding with the interview, but making decisions in the heat of the moment can often look wrong in hindsight. The clear conclusion was that Mr Russet presented a high risk and protective action was needed for the children in the family.

The problem of child sexual abuse is now more in the open, but it is thought to be far greater than reported, as it is difficult for adults, let alone children, to disclose it. I once had the awful experience of holding an eleven-year-old girl's hand as she was put through the ordeal of sitting in a huge court room in front of a bewigged judge and barristers. She was being asked to give evidence of her sexual abuse by her stepfather, who was present and sitting not far from her.

Several professionals had tried hard to prepare her. The judge also gave special permission for me to sit with her quietly in the court room by way of support. Nevertheless, the white-faced little girl managed to get as far as confirming her name in a small voice before a barrister's suggestion that her cross-examination be abandoned was accepted by the judge. The trial collapsed.

There must have been some corroborative evidence of the abuse having taken place, as a child's evidence does not reach trial if it is simply her, or his, evidence against a denial by the alleged perpetrator. The police would have investigated the allegation and, in this case, found evidence that satisfied the Crown Prosecution Service that a trial should take place. This can sometimes be medical evidence resulting from examination of the child, although I do not remember if that was what had led to this prosecution.

Systems have greatly improved, with specially trained professionals video-recording the child's evidence as soon as possible after it is first disclosed, avoiding "leading" (suggestive) questions. This would then be admitted as the child's primary evidence in court. In addition, the use of video suites means the child is no longer required to sit in the court room or see the alleged perpetrator during cross examination.

Nevertheless, getting strong enough evidence to pass the "beyond reasonable doubt" threshold required for a conviction remains very difficult. Happily, the family courts require only an "on balance of probability" threshold to protect children. Nevertheless, there is considerable injustice in the victims being removed from the family rather than the perpetrator, which has often been the only way to protect them.

The child's ability to manage these situations depends so much on the response of the non-abusing parent, often the mother. Many of them immediately put in place protective measures, evicting the alleged perpetrator, whilst several others refuse to believe the child's allegations, leaving agencies to take protective measures.

Another major factor is the child's resilience. I recall another eleven-year-old girl making a very clear disclosure in her video interview of abuse over some years. This included the fact that her stepfather had cut her toe a little with a Stanley knife, telling her that this would be what happened to her throat if she disclosed the abuse. Her mother immediately evicted her partner. Later, the girl said to me that she did not need any of the therapeutic work that I was offering to arrange for her, because her sole aim was to have the abuse stop. She was fine now, thanks, she said.

By contrast I had to do several sessions of supportive work with another young lad, despite the fact that he had suffered only a brief threat of being touched inappropriately by a stranger in a park. I do believe that a major factor in this lad's low resilience was his mother's huge anxiety about the incident, and her struggle to cope with this.

The explosive impact on families of disclosure of child sexual abuse means that it is likely that this scourge will continue to be largely hidden. Very sadly, many children will disclose such abuse, but it is taken no further by the adult to whom the disclosure is made for fear of the consequences for the family.

Chapter 4

Work with middle-class families

❧ ——— ✦ ——— ❧

It may come as no surprise that the bulk of social workers' intervention is with disadvantaged families. There are several factors at play here. A large majority of parents in such families have had abusive and/or deprived childhoods. This can result in an unsettled adulthood, with a struggle to form stable relationships. Another obvious factor is that the lack of resources available to them, including financial ones, as well as dependable family support results in them falling back on the statutory agencies.

Of course, abuse is by no means confined to such families. I have found, though, that work with relatively well-off families can present a particular challenge to social workers.

Many of the families with whom social workers work have had previous experience of, or at least some knowledge of, the world of social work and the statutory agencies' involvement in general. A quote I saw in one newly qualified social worker's write-up of an interview with a client has always made me a smile. The client said to her, "Don't try and tell me anything about social work. I've had social workers all my life!"

More "middle class" families are often less familiar with social work interventions and are ready to challenge more robustly any attempts to interfere in their lives. One such difficult case I had was during my work in South Africa. Sally was fifteen years old. Her father had died a couple of years previously, and she and her mother were the sole occupants of a large house in a quiet cul-de-sac located in a well-to-do area of the town I worked in.

Sally's mother had reacted badly to the death of her husband and was rather erratic and unpredictable emotionally. Mother-daughter relationships can often be strained during the teenage years, but Sally was really struggling with living with her mother and she decided to run away. The problem was that she ran away all of 500 yards or so to the end of the cul-de-sac where her best friend lived. The parents of her best friend were familiar with her mother's erratic emotions and decided that Sally could remain in their care for as long as she wanted to.

My involvement began because her mother contacted the police and asked them to use their authority to have her daughter return to her care. The police had been unable to persuade Sally to move and they passed the matter onto us.

Sally was equally clear to me that she had no intention of returning home. Her mother was very agitated with me when I visited her and could not understand why agencies felt unable to enforce her right to have her daughter in her care.

In England, the courts have long been guided by what is termed the Gillick Principle. There was a House of Lords ruling in 1981 in a case where Victoria Gillick had sought assurance from the local authority that contraceptive advice would not be given to her daughters without her consent. The local authority refused. The court ruling was that children below the age of sixteen, though still children in the eyes of the law, could be deemed to have developed sufficient maturity and understanding for parental consent not to be required in all areas of their lives.

This principle predates my involvement with Sally

and would not have applied there anyway. So Sally was effectively a child and it would require a court to decide whether the child had sufficient understanding to determine her own future, at least until she turned sixteen, when she could leave home of her own volition.

The ripples through the community were massive and I was given to understand that the GP practice of Sally and her family almost broke up over disagreement about what should happen. Many thought that Sally should, in effect, be given a hiding and told to go back home! Others were very much on the side of Sally and the family who were caring for her.

The court system that existed in those days in South Africa was significantly different from the current court procedures in England. Here, there is a Legal Aid system that automatically covers the expenses of both the child and the parents when the Family Court becomes involved. The child also has his or her own solicitor, and a Guardian, who is a social worker from an agency independent of the local authority bringing the proceedings.

This system carefully seeks to ensure that all the parties have their own say in court. Where the child is too young to express their own opinion, the Guardian is there to act independently on their behalf.

In South Africa at the time, the system was that the

social worker produced a report, and this was the prime evidence before the court. The hearing would be held in the office of the Commissioner for Child Welfare rather than a court room, to try to emphasise the relatively informal nature of the proceedings. The Commissioner would then take the parents through the social worker's report and get their views on the parts that they either agreed with or wished to challenge, before determining the outcome. Proceedings would therefore not take very long – perhaps an hour or two at the most.

Looking back, this gave great power to social workers. Often the social worker would be relatively articulate compared with the parents, familiar with the court milieu, and more often than not known to the Commissioner. The Commissioner would attempt to be as impartial as possible, and was permitted to give assistance to the parents in articulating their views. Nevertheless, in my experience almost invariably the social worker would come away with the court order he or she was recommending.

Diverging briefly from Sally, this relative imbalance of power came home to me most starkly in a case I dealt with at one point in South Africa, a case involving a family of Portuguese immigrants. I saw young Miguel on just three occasions before having the court make an order that sent him off to a School of Industries hundreds of miles away.

The family was referred by a school which was concerned at his frequent absences. They came into my office: two parents who were unable to speak English or Afrikaans, with Miguel and his slightly younger sister. She it was who acted as interpreter for the parents – in itself a highly questionable way of conducting an interview.

The parents spoke of Miguel being essentially beyond their control, which was one of the criteria that could enable a court to make a care order, enabling his removal from their care. He would go out without permission, return home late and often refuse to attend school.

Essentially, all I could do was to explain to him the risk that he was running of being sent to a School of Industries, which as I have previously explained was the only resource open to us in those days for older children who could not be cared for by family members.

I arranged a further interview with him on his own, and again pressed this line with him when he was unable or unwilling to give any good explanation for his behaviour. Shortly after he left the office, I received a call from a shop around the corner. The owner had learned that Miguel had just left my office, and he had been caught shoplifting. I asked for him to be returned to my office.

I then told him he had given me no choice other than to seek an order from the court.

I was amazed when I came to England at how tolerant society was of youngsters going off the rails in this way and how many chances they were given to alter their behaviour. I got frustrated and perplexed at times whilst I adjusted to this new regime, having found it so easy in South Africa to intervene in an authoritative manner. In England I would have thoughts such as, "What more does this child need to do to take more drastic action to curb his behaviour?"

The answer is that there are a number of options available here by way of support services to the family, diversionary activities for bored youngsters and alternative educational facilities. All are aimed to avoid, if possible, the drastic step of their removal from home.

So, a court order on Miguel almost inevitably followed. I often wonder how he fared at a School of Industries so far from home, in an area where Afrikaans was far more dominant than English. I believe he was only one of four English speakers in the school.

* * *

Returning now to Sally, her court case was the first

and, in fact the only, time I was faced in South Africa with a solicitor representing the parent. I underwent quite confrontational cross-examination. The solicitor would have had little or no experience of working in a Family Court and essentially used the same tactics as he would have done in a criminal trial. His argument was that teenage children are often difficult to manage and oppositional towards their parents. He sought to present Sally's behaviour therefore as a common feature of children of her age and that a mother has the right to deal with that behaviour, within reason, in the way that she chooses rather than be faced with the removal of the child from her care.

One of the solicitor's tactics was to extract quotations that supported this argument from a book on psychology. At one point, he suddenly decided to ask me how many names of the contributors to the book I recognised. Each name he read out I had to admit was unfamiliar to me, until he came to the name Anna Freud and I professed to knowing her name!

In criminal courts, I believe, a tactic that solicitors and barristers may often use in cross-examination is to discredit the person being cross-examined, to undermine their evidence. The solicitor in Sally's case was quite derisory in his tone with me, referring a few times in a rather sneering way to my "vast" two-and-a-half years' experience. "So you" he would say, "with your vast two-and-a-half years' experience, deign to tell me that my client..." and so on. In the same tone, he expressed amazement that I had heard of one of the names of the contributors to the book.

The case was adjourned for lunch, and it speaks volumes in regard to the type of case I was dealing with that Sally's carers invited me to join them for lunch at a fairly exclusive club in the town. Embarrassingly for all concerned, a few tables away sat Sally's mother and solicitor.

On return to court, the Commissioner announced that he had decided to adjourn the case for a time, instructing the solicitor to seek a psychiatrist who could provide a report to the court after seeing Sally and her mother. And so, proceedings came abruptly to an end.

In the ensuing days, I talked with my supervisor about my concern that Sally was having to listen to all this. Being the age she was, she was present throughout the hearing. My supervisor agreed to write to the Commissioner and express a view that Sally should be excluded for the rest of the hearing when it recommenced, other than to give her own evidence in need, although it would be highly unlikely that the court would require her to do so.

The Commissioner responded, copying in the solicitor and expressing his support of this view. However, he included in his letter a view that the solicitor was seeking to prove that I was not a psychologist, which I had not claimed to be. He went further, stating that, in his view on the evidence thus far, Sally should be declared a Child in need of Care (the equivalent then of a care order). The solicitor's response was that this was evidence that the Commissioner had made up his mind about the outcome before hearing all the evidence, and appealed this matter to a higher court.

What a mess! It took almost a year for the case to come before the higher court, which ordered the Commissioner to recuse himself and for a new Commissioner to hear the case. By this stage, the Commissioner concerned had retired anyway.

I recall shortly afterwards speaking to the new Commissioner about the matter. He noted that Sally would be turning sixteen in a few weeks, and thus free legally to determine where she lived. He decided to continue to adjourn the case for those few weeks and then to close it.

I went to say my farewell to Sally after she turned sixteen. She was still living with her friends and doing well. A travesty of justice? Quite possibly so, although

I cannot think of another outcome for Sally other than being dragged kicking and screaming back to her mother's care.

* * *

I was involved in another fraught and very sad case in my later career in England with a reasonably well-off, well-educated family, again involving a fifteen-year-old girl leaving home against her parents' wishes. Cindy insisted that her father was making inappropriate sexual advances to her, although she never made allegations of actually being abused. Her father vehemently denied the allegations. Cindy remained adamant that she wanted to go into foster care, as she felt unsafe in her father's care.

A memory I have that emphasised how different it was to be working with middle-class families is that Cindy, during her time in care, gave me a Christmas present of a pair of socks she had bought for me from her pocket money. I was so touched. I had to declare the gift to management: it is not appropriate to be accepting gifts from clients. Happily, management did not consider that a pair of socks constituted sufficient evidence, if it ever came to light, that I was being bribed!

Intensive investigation and work with the family got no further than this. Cindy's mother strongly took her husband's side, and interviews with the younger children revealed nothing of concern. They were perfectly happy to remain in their parents' care.

Friends rallying round to take sides was a feature of both Sally and Cindy's cases. Cindy's court case was a long drawn-out and painful affair with a number of witnesses coming forward for the parents. All gave evidence that both parents were loving and entirely appropriate, as far as they were concerned, in their care of the children. It ended with the court refusing to make a Care Order, thus requiring that Cindy should return home. The problem was how to persuade her, after she had throughout her stay in foster care insisted that she would not return.

It was agreed that I should organise for Cindy to meet her mother in "neutral" territory. A café was chosen, and a quiet spot sought. It had been made clear that as the court had made no order over her, I would be taking a back seat and leaving her mother to tell her she must return home. Of course, Cindy had been told of the court's decision before this meeting took place.

Cindy nevertheless continued her strong resistance, and in fact said that she would jump out of a window to escape if she were forced to go home. Her mother was, of course, terribly upset despite Cindy's insistence that she loved her and missed her siblings: she just really could not feel safe, she said, in the care of her father.

It was a sad outcome for a very unhappy family. Cindy, however, continued to do well at school and remained in foster care until she was able to move on to supported independence.

But it was an even sadder ending, as I learned that, at the age of seventeen, Cindy took her own life. I had no other details. I can only surmise that, struggling to achieve independent living without her family's support and perhaps with some continued pressure on her to change her stance regarding her father, she could see no other way out of her unhappiness.

I have noticed in my career that girls who in their teenage years have had a fraught relationship with their mother, to the point where their leaving home is the only option, often had a reasonable, or even a good, relationship with her once they were not living together. I hope that in time, Sally was able to do so. I wish the same had been possible for Cindy.

It strikes me that I have been aware of the deaths of young people an awful lot. I had already encountered tragic death during my time in army training, although that involved an adult. My platoon was on an early-morning run when we came across a car with its engine running and a hosepipe leading from its exhaust into the car. My colleagues tried the doors, but they were locked. I picked up a brick from a neighbouring garden and smashed the back window. The smell of the exhaust fumes that hit me remained with me for many years. The make of petrol that was common in that region had a particular odour and whenever I went back there it would trigger an unpleasant memory of this encounter with death.

There was a man on the back seat with his arm crooked in a way that made it evident that he had been holding the hosepipe in his mouth, although it had slipped out of his hand by then. He appeared to be in his early forties, or thereabouts. I felt for a pulse, but the absence of one, and the fact that his arm returned to its original position when I let go, made it evident that he had been dead for some time already.

Later that day I was required to go to the police station to identify the body. I also formed part of the Guard of Honour at the funeral, where we fired three shots over his coffin as he was lowered into the ground. I learned nothing more about him other than that he was a member of the armed forces who suffered from depression. He must have been a lonely man. To me, the absence of a family member to identify his body and the fact that a group of trainees unknown to him were forming his Guard of Honour make this particularly poignant.

Looking back, I am surprised at how little I was affected by the experience at the time, although on my return from identifying the body I learned from my sergeant major that I had been given five days' home leave to recover! I was not aware of feeling any significant reaction. I was only a teenager though, and I know that back then I could be insensitive.

Returning to my social work career, in addition to Cindy, I heard of the suicide of a very likeable girl I had got to know during my stint of working in residential care, which I will deal with later. She apparently jumped from the roof of a multi-storey car park a year or two after gaining independence. The transition to independence is a highly vulnerable time for young people leaving care.

I had a very brief involvement with a lad of about seven years and his mother. I did a one-off visit by way of introduction, as the pair of them had just moved into the area from elsewhere, but there had been concerns for the lad's well-being. The lad was subject to a Child Protection Plan or its equivalent at the time, and a transfer case conference was being arranged.

They were temporarily housed in a large Victorian building let out as flats. They were on the third floor.

On the night of my visit there was a fire in the building and, with no working smoke alarms, the pair of them succumbed. I had only met them for perhaps less than an hour, but of course I was deeply affected.

A client I knew far better was Edith. She and her sister had been in the sole care of their father for a few years following their mother's death. Unlike her sister, Edith struggled to comply with her father's wishes, and she became a rebellious teenager. Finally, her father requested that she be placed in foster care. I was involved with Edith for a year or two in foster care. She continued to struggle to settle and, as soon as she was old enough, she jumped at the chance of being placed in independent living.

This was in an age when the UK had a very high incidence of teenage pregnancy and I recall thinking that I could count on one hand the number of girls I knew who were not pregnant when they left care. Being in care is always a huge disruption in a child's life, no matter how skilled his or her carers might be, and so many young women said that they were pleased to be pregnant because they felt this was the one opportunity they had to love and be loved unconditionally. They were just not mature enough, nor did they have enough by way of alternative hopeful prospects elsewhere, to understand the difficulties that can arise caring for a baby as a single young parent.

The deaths of Edith and her unborn child were particularly traumatic. Their bodies were found in a burnt-out flat that Edith was occupying. It was apparently evident that she was murdered before the fire was started.

My manager was not a callous person by any means, but his reaction was particularly striking. He asked for the file and my write-ups of visits I had made to Edith, and on returning the file he looked pleased and said he thought we had "covered ourselves" or something similar – I do not recall his exact words. I do recall feeling devastated, having known Edith so well. I was taken aback by my manager's reaction, despite understanding that, from the organisation's point of view, the greatest fear was the press getting hold of information that young Edith and her unborn child had not received at least the level of support that was statutorily required of Social Services.

Although Edith and her father had fallen out, he was both devastated and understandably angry with whoever had done this. The police quickly apprehended Edith's boyfriend. The trial was apparently a short one, Edith's father told me, because the boyfriend admitted having been heavily under the influence of alcohol and drugs, and during an argument he had seen Edith as a witch.

He had stabbed her several times before setting fire to her bed to try to hide the evidence. Oh, how very sad.

Chapter 5

Residential social work

In 1980, after five years of practice in South Africa, I moved to England. I found two positions open to me after interview, and chose a residential setting, as this offered a change from my previous experience and therefore a new challenge. It proved a short sojourn in residential social work, and I thought I would write briefly about this, chiefly as a salute to those who work in this arena.

Because of my qualification and experience I was given a position as Team Leader. It did not take me long to learn that qualification and experience as a social worker do not of themselves make one fit to lead a team of residential workers.

The place where I worked was called an Assessment Centre, run by the local authority, and consisted of two units of about twelve beds each. The aim was to have teenagers who had difficulties placed there on a temporary basis whilst assessment of their needs took place to assist in determining where best to place them in the longer term.

The overall manager was on long-term sick leave and the centre was run by the two assistant managers, each in overall charge of a unit. This made things difficult. Both managers were experienced and competent leaders, but they had different ideas regarding how their unit should be run. One favoured the overall strategy of staff members using their relationships with the young people to influence them into improving their behaviour and well-being. The other argued that what they had thus far lacked was structure and consistent discipline in their lives. Providing this would give a safe environment for the youngsters to feel secure enough to modify their behaviour. Firm authority was more of the ethos than building surrogate-parent-style relationships.

I was in no position to argue one way or the other: both units, it seemed to me, had their successes with some youngsters and failures with others. Difficulties could arise, however, at times as the managers alternated in being in overall charge over nights and weekends. When called upon for advice or to attend in managing a difficult situation, a clash of these philosophies could become evident.

But the overall problem with whole setup was primarily the placement of youngsters with different problems, and different degrees of problematic behaviour, together in relatively large units. The fact that some of them still attended school outside the centre and required good routines and sleep did not sit comfortably with some of the more disruptive youngsters, who on occasion caused major disturbances that could go on into the early hours. The local authority closed the centre within eighteen months of my starting work there.

My own lesson, which, as I have said, was learned quite early on, came within a few months when I was deemed able to have the more experienced workers in my team move into other teams whilst I took on a role of bringing on new workers. I soon learned that trying to exert firm control over a disruptive group of teenagers can quickly turn into a game of cat and mouse for them. On occasion, fortunately rare, we would have to enlist the assistance of the police to regain control.

This loss of control thankfully did not invariably fall on my shift. Nevertheless, after it had occurred a few times on my watch, I persuaded managers to allocate one or two experienced workers back on my team. An effective method I learned through this was to indicate to the disruptive youngsters that we were aware of their behaviour, but then to ignore them for some time before again intervening. They would often then tire of the behaviour and not turn it into a game.

I do not want to be too negative: we had good times and provided a reasonably safe environment generally whilst we sought the right sort of longer-term placement for them. In a number of cases, though, there were not suitable alternatives available and some of the youngsters remained placed with us until they achieved independence, or the centre was closed and they moved to alternative provision in the area.

My time there coincided with a period when a few disruptive young people were finding release, or at least temporary fun, in the practice of glue sniffing. One of the less savoury memories I have is of looking for and disposing of plastic bags full of glue that some of them were inhaling deeply and getting a real high from. This was a much cheaper option for them than alcohol, and I recall no problems with dealing with alcohol consumption, thank goodness. The effects of glue sniffing were far more short-lived and never to my recall associated with increased aggression, as drunkenness could have been.

About a year after the centre's closure I was briefly

involved with a young man aged seventeen who had attempted to move on to independent living, but had difficulty with this. One evening he broke into the unit in which he had previously been resident and spent the night in his old haunts. He was arrested and charged with breaking and entering.

He had been one of the long-term residents in the unit and was on the whole one of the least disruptive elements. I had great empathy with him wanting to return to the place where he had lived for a few years, even though it was empty. I was frankly shocked when I accompanied him to court to face the charges and the magistrates said that they had instructions to clamp down on a spate of breaking and entering that was occurring at the time. They therefore sentenced him to three months in a Youth Offenders' Institute.

What a tragedy, I felt. Nothing would be more likely to steer him in the direction of further crime. He did not enter the premises to steal. I hope he managed as he grew older to settle and find stability in his life.

As I have indicated, I have huge admiration for, and want to pay tribute to, those who work in residential units trying to help youngsters through difficult times. This goes for many devoted foster carers, too. On numerous occasions I have placed disturbed children with them and quietly felt thankful to be leaving the foster carers to manage them on a 24/7 basis!

I suppose it's "each to their own" so to speak, as sometimes when I said this to foster carers, I would get the response that they were only too pleased not to be a social worker! They felt more comfortable with looking after disrupted children than being responsible for the long-term major decisions for the children's future, and dealing with difficult parents.

I have to say that my brief spell in residential social work dented my confidence for a time and it was one of several experiences I had over the years that had the effect of pulling me up short. I was over-confident as a young man and at various times I had to learn what my shortcomings were, and to face them. It certainly taught me that having a degree in social work does not of itself provide all the skills necessary to manage a team of colleagues or, indeed, a group of unruly teenagers!

Chapter 6

Generic or specialised?

It took just eighteen months after my arrival for the decision to be made to close the assessment centre. That heralded the first of a few episodes in my career where I was put back into the front line of social work, working directly with children and families.

I came to England in 1980 shortly after a significant government inquiry into the provision of social services and was told that the Seebohm Report had led to a complete reordering. I gathered that the primary thrust of the report's findings was that services were fragmented, and responsibilities were shared amongst various government departments. Rather than several specialisms, services to families should be provided by generic social workers, working with people from cradle to grave under the auspices of a single government department, Social Services.

Services were provided by "Patch Teams" in my local authority – teams responsible for specific geographical areas. I worked primarily with older children in South Africa and in the assessment centre. Now I would additionally be working with young children, children with disabilities and the elderly.

The reality was, however, that when it came to allocation meetings social workers took on cases that seemed to be within the remit of their expertise and interest. I do not recall any elderly people on my caseload, as they tended to be taken on by one or two workers who far preferred working with them to working with "problem" families.

On the other hand, allocation meetings could be like drawing teeth. It was far more common for social workers to feel – often quite rightly – that they had too many cases already. The manager would then have to put pressure on their staff or, if there really was too much for the team to take on, to decide which matters needed the most urgent attention. Allocation meetings were never the favourite time of the week for social workers!

I will mention one stark difference I encountered on coming to England, that of funding. In South Africa, all statutory services were provided by central government and there were therefore no problems in using services provided in a different province.

I had to learn the vagaries of local authority funding here. Decisions about one's clients on occasion could be complicated by families moving from or to other areas, or services required existing in another area. Negotiations could be difficult, with cash-strapped local authorities fiercely defending their finances. On occasions the courts could become involved in determining where the family is "normally resident" and therefore which local authority is financially responsible. Such complications could be highly frustrating.

It struck me that cases often turned out less dreadful than they sounded at first reading. I well recall a time when I changed teams, for reasons I need not go into here. I sat at my new desk reading the first six files I had been given, feeling despair. All were long-term cases – families with intractable problems that had been open for months or even years. Reading the files felt ever more disheartening given the long history of difficulties and the long-term nature of these problems.

I was aware a few weeks later, though, that I had developed a different attitude once I had met the families. The problems were still evident, and apparently intractable, but somehow the cases had become more humanised to me and things did not look so bleak once faces were put to names. They were still bleak, but I felt less disheartened.

Perhaps inevitably, there were some visits that had to be made that felt less daunting than others. Social work is subject to a lot of regulation in England, as no doubt it is elsewhere. There are requirements on statutory social work agencies to visit most cases at a minimum frequency that is laid down. For example, children who were on the Child Protection Register (in my early days) or more latterly termed subject to a Child Protection Plan, had to be visited at least on a fortnightly basis.

One of the families I found difficult to visit was one with a father from an Arab country who seemed to fit the profile of a culture in which the man is autocratic and cannot be questioned. Mr Hussein was polite with me, although in a rather patronising and condescending way. My visits were tolerated. Just.

I recall a visit where, I think, some allegation had been made of his punishing a child too severely. He summoned the children and the four of them stood in a line in front of us, for all intents and purposes looking like a line of soldiers standing to attention in front of their sergeant major, and ordered to make their bodies available to me for examination for bruises or marks. I declined the invitation! It would have been highly inappropriate for me to do so unless such bruises or marks were readily visible on exposed parts of the body. In any case, such examinations would only lead to appropriate evidence if a doctor or paediatrician carried them out.

Action to protect children is naturally governed carefully through legislation. I felt that I could lay a bet on abuse occurring within this family, but evidence is necessary to take action. Even when a child alleges sexual abuse, as occurred at one point in the Hussein family, this can lead to a case conference and the child or children becoming subject to Child Protection Plans, but if it is the child's word against a denial by the father (as occurred here), legal action is difficult without further evidence.

I tried working with the British mother of this family, but Mrs Hussein was either too fearful or too loyal to say anything against her husband. I had an interesting and salutary experience with her. I do not recall the exact details, but the matter did lead on to court proceedings at one point. As far as I can remember, the mother was fighting against the removal of the children from her care, based on her saying that she had separated from her husband and was protecting them from seeing him. I suspected that she was still allowing him to visit.

In any case, it was a court hearing that required evidence to be heard but, for the one and only time in my career, every effort to have a solicitor available to attend to argue the local authority's case was unsuccessful. I had therefore to cross-examine the mother when she was in the witness box. Solicitors are, of course, trained and skilled in this.

I felt I knew enough about court procedures, having undergone cross-examination, as well as witnessing cross-examination, very many times in my career. I had to put some challenging questions to Mrs Hussein. She was successful in keeping the children in her care, at least for the time being.

I then tried to resume my role as social worker to the family, but on my next visit I was met with her leaning out of the window, screaming at me and vowing never to let me cross the threshold again! My spell in the role of cross-examiner had left her convinced that I was highly biased, as she did not like some of the questions I had put to her. It seems obvious that this was going to be the result and clearly it had been inappropriate for me to step outside my role. It took me some time to be allowed into the home again.

Later in the history of the Hussein family, the children

were removed, but by then the case was in the hands of another social worker, as I had moved on. I know this, because some years later I happened to chair the final review meeting regarding the girl in this family.

When children are in care, review meetings must be held on a regular basis to review the child's progress and the arrangements for care, contact with parents and so on. This young woman had reached the age when she would no longer be in care, and in fact she was already living in independent accommodation and had a child. (Another teenage pregnancy!) She looked at me somewhat wistfully and said, "I did tell you that I was being sexually abused, didn't I?"

I could only acknowledge this, apologise sincerely, and say that I was powerless to do anything about it without more evidence, as the investigation had produced nothing other than a denial by her father. Happily, she seemed to be aware of this, or at least accepted my word that I had not been legally able to protect her at that stage, and the rest of the review was a positive one as she was doing very well.

I do hope she continued to do well. Sexual abuse can have a devastating effect on victims. I mentioned earlier that some children have remarkable resilience, but there is a great deal of evidence of the high prevalence of victims of sexual abuse having mental health and drug problems later in life.

* * *

As with any profession, much of social work is routine. There is concern about how much time is spent in front of computers rather than visiting families. It has felt over the years that this has increased, but I recall being taken aback in my university days reading of studies, way back then that found that social workers spent very little time carrying out their duties with families as opposed to fulfilling more bureaucratic duties.

When I started work in a local authority team in England, I recall doing case notes (records of visits and so on) using a Dictaphone. Each team had its administrative team who transferred these onto computers. These days, of course, we write such things directly onto the computers that are on every desk.

Even the visits to families could be routine, to a certain extent. As an example, children in settled placements might need the required statutory visit to make sure everything was continuing to go well for them. Of course, such visits are important, but very often there were no real surprises awaiting me.

Even families where the children were still present could become rather predictable, if the main purpose was to provide regular support. I remember one mother being so used to me visiting her and the children that I found her playing games on her computer during my visit. This gave every indication that my visits were not having much impact!

But there were times of high drama. Primarily, this has involved the removal of children, which can be dramatic as well as traumatic. I have thankfully never been involved in this without feeling convinced that it was the right decision for the children's welfare – or at least as convinced as I could be. No one can predict the future and there is sometimes – and should be – some lingering doubt about whether one's predictions of harm for the children are justified or not. However, of course such decisions are taken very seriously and not – even back then in South Africa – taken on one's own. There is always, at the least, consultation with a manager and often confirmation by a court must follow.

Most of the time in any case the decision is not needed as an emergency and the courts will be involved, with the parents having the opportunity to oppose the decision.

In fact, it would be a senior police officer who would make the decision in an emergency and, again as in South Africa, the decision would have to be swiftly sanctioned by the court.

The local authority can approach a judge in order to make an emergency decision. Sometimes this could be taken without the parent having the opportunity to oppose it at that stage if the decision were deemed sufficiently urgent, or particularly if the parent or parents were themselves accused of abuse. In such a case, parents will within a short time be represented at a further hearing in the court to seek the return of the child or children.

In situations of high drama, one can be at risk of assault. I have thankfully been involved in very little by way of violence. Where violence, or the possibility of violence, can be predicted, working alongside the police is an obvious way to protect the social worker.

One situation I faced was when, as a senior social worker, I accompanied a social worker who was having to visit a home to remove the children on the decision of a judge. We had the police present. On the door being answered, an angry mother pointed at me. She accused me of having wanted to take her children away from her for a long time. I realised later why I was being accused of this: as the social worker's supervisor I had on a few occasions been present to back her up when she had to confront the family about allegations. I was seen particularly therefore as the bringer of bad news.

The mother happened to have a man present, a friend, who was clearly a large bodybuilder. This man appeared in the doorway, his heaving tattooed torso covered only in a vest, which did not hide his bulging neck and muscles. He took the mother's identification of me as the primary cause of her distress as a prompt to take me into an adjoining passageway and have me pinned against the wall. He was voicing threats and making punching movements at my chest, obviously ready to do me serious harm.

I wondered where the police were, but they were busy with the social worker and mother. The local authority provided training for us in dealing with violence, but in my experience, it is hard to recall training in such situations! Happily, on this occasion, my lack of resistance seemed to work. I maintained a relaxed stance, open-handed, and quietly spoke of the futility of taking things out on me. I cannot remember what I said, but it was likely to be soothing talk of the mother's right to have things reviewed quickly in court. He did after a while let me go and turned his attention to loud goings-on nearby.

I gathered later that a police officer suffered a similar assault to mine and the man was swiftly arrested: it seemed to me that threatening a police officer was deemed more serious than assault on a social worker! No, I do not mean that: it is likely that what happened to me was missed in the maelstrom. In the end, the mother was also arrested, I think for breach of the peace, and we were left to gather the children and take them to their foster placement.

* * *

Having mentioned that one does not always remember training tips when in a situation of threat, I recall an incident in which my reaction was very much contrary to what any trainer would recommend. I visited a home to inform parents that if they continued to befriend a man recently released from prison after serving time for a sex offence against a child, I would be convening a child protection case conference to review how the children could be protected.

Unfortunately, the man in question was present. With hindsight, perhaps I should have insisted on seeing the parents on their own, but they said they felt that he should be present to hear what I had to say. I thought, too, that this would assist them by making it clear that the impetus for his removal was not coming from them.

Another problem was that I was sitting in a large, low, comfortable armchair and therefore potentially in a difficult position to defend myself. After I had conveyed my message, the offender got up from his chair and came over to me, looming over me, angrily shaking his fist in my face, and declaring that he had done his time and was sick of having his offence (which he denied having committed) continually brought up.

My reaction should have been non-retaliatory. Taking a "one-down" position, open-handed, speaking quietly – I think all these would have been more appropriate. Instead, though, I momentarily lost my temper and, despite being in a low chair, managed to rise from it and put my finger in his face, declaring I was not there to take nonsense (or similar) from him. I am well aware that this action would most likely increase tension. I am just very lucky that I quickly got control of myself and caught myself saying "If you carry on like this, I'll..." and after a moment's pause, moved my finger to point to the door and say "... I'll walk out now"!

By this stage, the father had stepped in and said, "Calm down, you two." The parents asked the man to leave and I was then able to explain more calmly to the parents about case conferences and child protection procedures, to help them make a decision. I seem to recall that they decided to end the friendship.

This was all before new procedures have enabled the courts to put such offenders on a Sex Offenders Register. Now, in such situations, a police officer responsible for monitoring such offenders should be available for a social worker to contact and possibly to co-work the case.

The only other significantly dangerous situation I can recall was on a visit to a father of children who were in care. I do not remember the details, but there were clearly problems over the way he was managing contact with the children. Again, I found myself in a low chair. I clearly had not learned from my previous experience of such chairs! The father became angry, got up and took some photos of his children in glass-fronted frames from the wall and began smashing them across his knee. He was close enough for me to find shards of glass landing all around me, in my lap, and alarmingly near my face.

This time, I was at least able to stay calm and to say to him that I wished to leave. He carried on ranting for a short time, but stepped away enough for me to be able to collect my things, to tell him that I would arrange a follow-up, and to leave. The next interview was by invitation at my office, a safer place for me than a home interview.

One quote I would never forget came from a stepfather I was visiting because of concerns over his handling of two children. He explained his tough disciplining stance by saying, "I remember my father hitting my naked brother with a chair leg around the floor of the kitchen until he shat himself. I used to hate him, but I now respect him because I realise he was just trying to teach us right from wrong."

I do not think he was intending to repeat the actions of his father on his stepchildren – at least, I hope not. Nevertheless, within a short space of time concerns for the children escalated sufficiently for me to remove them. This was one of the very few occasions I got to know the outcome. I met this man's stepson at a time when he was about to leave care and I was able to ask him if he thought the right decision had been made to put him in care. The answer was an emphatic yes.

It has surprised me that some mothers choose to continue their relationship with an abusive man over keeping the children in their care, but I have come across this all too often in my career, sadly. Such men are often very controlling, and it might be out of fear that such mothers remain in the relationship. Often it is out of financial dependence. There must be numerous reasons.

I had one mother discuss her dilemma with me during an interview. Her fifteen-year-old daughter was making clear allegations of sexual abuse by her stepfather. The mother was unsure whether to believe her or her husband's denial. She told me she was faced with a choice between a man who was bringing in a steady income and the promise of a continued stable relationship, and a difficult, argumentative daughter who was vowing to leave home as soon as she turned sixteen. She chose to put her daughter into care – another case of a victim unjustly having to leave the family instead of the perpetrator.

Social workers work in risky situations and need always to assess as best they can the risks they are facing or likely to face. In my experience, managers are very aware of this and there are cases where visits are always made jointly with a colleague.

At one stage in my career, I was surprised to hear managers say that we could terminate abusive telephone calls. It made me rethink my stance on this. In training to become a social worker, we are told that we should be empathetic and non-judgmental and to build relationships. This, together with social workers being in the profession because of a desire to help, indicated to me that it would help my client if I heard them out and tried to express my understanding of their situation, even if they were being abusive.

Of course, managers in fields other than social work are also acutely aware of this and one can see notices in many offices, shops, hospitals and so on which indicate that abusive behaviour to staff will not be tolerated. I am surprised now that it had to be pointed out to me that I did not have to tolerate abuse, even if I was safely at the end of a telephone line. I learned that being clear about my intention to terminate the call, or even doing so, did not ultimately adversely affect my relationship with the client concerned once they calmed down.

I can be thankful that over a lengthy career the worst injury I ever suffered was perhaps injury to my pride, such as standing helplessly whilst my chest was being gently pounded in accompaniment with dire threats to my general well-being. However empathetic a social worker tries to be with people having children removed from their care or similar, the motivation is always to protect the children from abuse and neglect, and violence cannot be tolerated.

Chapter 7

Any alternatives?

I continued working in front-line teams for about sixteen years. Such work with families can be stressful. Even routine visits could be difficult, knowing the family is accepting your visit under sufferance and can at times be downright hostile.

As with workers in any stressful occupation, "work/life balance" is important. These days it is easy to take work home with you – literally, as working from home can be a useful way of getting reports written and avoiding distractions in the office.

Earlier in my career this was not possible: home computers were not available, or compatible with office work. Case notes (records of each visit, telephone call, meeting etc.) and reports were written in longhand or dictated for office staff to type up. Nothing could stop you, though, from taking worries home, and many a night's sleep was disturbed. This impacts on family life, and stresses within the family can add to the difficulties. I was blessed with a stable family life, but my wife had stressful work as a nurse as well as health difficulties, and the strains can put relationships very much to the test.

My outlets were music and church. Such distractions from allowing pressures of work to dominate one's life are so important. Having spent my life as part of the Christian community, I have found church playing a stabilising, generally reassuring, role for me. When faced with stressful times and difficult decisions I found myself praying that the outcome would be the best possible option for the children concerned. Of course, I have no means of knowing what influence that had, if any, but it provided some comfort for me to think that there might be a benign influence overseeing proceedings.

At various points in my career I tried to escape from this front-line work with children and families. However, it has been a feature of my career, and perhaps it is evidence of the desperation that local authorities experience in filling vacancies in this important work, that I usually landed up back in such a post.

I have written of my first attempt at doing something else when I tried my hand at residential social work. As I related, this lasted only some eighteen months before the centre was closed down and I returned to a team working "in the field", as the front-line work is occasionally called.

Sometimes, seeking a change has instead been to pursue options open to me whilst continuing primarily with the work with children and families. One such option was training to work alongside the police in conducting what are now termed Achieving Best Evidence (ABE) interviews with children who were alleging abuse.

I previously mentioned the eleven-year-old girl whose hand I held whilst she tried, but failed, to repeat her allegations and face cross-examination in a highly intimidating High Court hearing. Concern about such situations gave rise to the ABE interviews, where the child's primary evidence was taken in a specially equipped video suite by trained workers. The child could, if necessary, still be required to face cross-examination in court, but such interviews could at least provide the initial evidence, and avoid the child having to retell the story on different occasions. Only if it went to full trial could the child face cross-examination, and that, these days, would be likely to be via video link.

Special training was given, as some specific court procedures were necessary, unlike ordinary social work interviews. Thus, after general chat to try to put the child at ease, such things as the names of those present would need to be established, and the time and date confirmed.

One further step was to seek to establish that the child understood what truth was and what was a lie. This was explored through a simple question, depending on the age of the child, such as giving the wrong colour of clothing worn and asking if that was the truth or a lie. The child would then be asked to confirm that they would tell only the truth in the interview. The child would be told that the interview was being video recorded. I previously mentioned a young girl who gave a clear interview in these circumstances, including saying that her toe had been slightly cut with a Stanley knife. She had also been warned that she would be hurt more severely if she ever revealed the abuse.

Many interviews, though, were far less straightforward, and several times would lead nowhere. The child might be unwilling to disclose abuse, or simply too young to understand what was wanted. They might be too fearful of the consequences of disclosure for them or their family, despite all the assurances that could be offered to them.

However, action to protect the child might still be possible, depending on what other evidence was available. The failure of the ABE interview would very probably rule out a criminal prosecution of the alleged perpetrator, because of the requirement in such trials to achieve the threshold of "beyond reasonable doubt". Proceedings in the Family Court to protect the child would be possible if the evidence was sufficient to pass the lower threshold of "on balance of probabilities".

Doing such interviews was a real challenge. As well as the child being exposed to critical analysis based on the video evidence, so were you, in terms of your interviewing techniques! As it turned out, though, in my experience most often the main interviewer was the police officer, who would be far more experienced in obtaining court evidence for possible prosecutions. My role then would be primarily as consultant, or quite often as the "third umpire" so to speak, operating the video recorder from behind a one-way mirror. At the end the interviewer would come through to ask if you thought everything had been covered before the interview was finally terminated.

A skill we were taught was not to ask leading questions. I was taught about this in my qualifying course, but it is particularly important in ABE interviews, as the child's response could be ruled as inadmissible if the question was deemed to lead the child towards a specific answer. It takes some thought, in the heat of the moment so to speak, to avoid a question such as, "Was his face angry when he did this?" rather than something like "What did his face look like when he did this?"

I remember one such interview with a lad of about five or six years of age. In fact, this one was carried out by two social workers, as no specific allegation had been made, but the lad's sexualised behaviour at school had for some time prompted concerns over whether he was being sexually abused. My female colleague took the lead in the interview and she made use of toys and anatomically correct dolls to try to get the lad to reveal any abuse he was suffering – always difficult when no specific allegation had been made, and without using leading questions.

The lad gave every indication of being comfortable with being interviewed, but we were getting nowhere. He started asking if he could show us his willy! Of course, my colleague refused the offer, and did so repeatedly. However, the lad was persistent. As with the dilemma I had felt over the man who had brought an axe into interview and refused to continue without the video being switched off, my colleague was faced with the dilemma over whether acceding to the lad's request might enable him finally to open up about what might be happening to him.

After a long period of getting nowhere, therefore, we agreed to him doing so, if only to make some progress, and the lad proudly and briefly displayed an erect penis. However, we continued to get nowhere in obtaining anything of concern and the interview was therefore terminated. Without any tangible evidence the social workers dealing with the lad could only continue to monitor his progress.

I found it frustrating when there were such concerns about a child but not enough evidence to take protective action. It was so difficult to resist the temptation to use leading questions. Doing so, however, would make any evidence obtained inadmissible in court and would therefore not help to protect the child.

In the 1980s and 1990s there was a wave of concern about child sexual abuse. Once the problem was out in the open, there was a sense that it was occurring everywhere, a hidden scourge that need to be rooted out. The use of anatomically correct dolls (dolls with breasts/penis and pubic hair as appropriate) was controversial, but was aimed to enable the child to talk about such things if they chose to do so. Again, care was taken not to lead the child, but to try to help him or her overcome any inhibitions by the interviewer asking, for example, in a neutral tone what the child called these parts of the human body.

After some time, sexual abuse issues quietened down. There had been a spate of adults feeling more comfortable about coming forward with historical concerns about having been abused. This accounted for a spike in such cases and legitimate concerns that this kind of abuse was far more prevalent than was evident at the time.

Social work with children moved on to focus more on other issues, and one that has been prominent in later decades has been the effects of domestic violence on children witnessing this.

Social workers in cases where there are concerns, but a lack of sufficient evidence to act, rely heavily on schoolteachers. Many worries about children are, of course, picked up in the schools where children spend significant periods of their lives. I did not have any follow up with the lad whose interview I described, but it is likely that social work involvement would have been terminated with an agreement with the school to refer any further concerns back again.

It sometimes requires several incidents – for instance, this lad was touching other children inappropriately at times – for the concern to reach the threshold where the courts could be approached to try to protect the child from whatever might be lying behind this behaviour.

* * *

Virtually the opposite from learning not to use leading questions, I learned a technique that can be used with sex offenders, or alleged sex offenders: that of assumptive questioning. An adult of average intelligence can counter a leading question. I have frequently felt critical of police on programmes such as Midsomer Murders for using leading questions! Equally though, many is the time when the person interviewed proves capable of dealing with the leading question through denial.

So, what is assumptive questioning? I have mentioned that one of my attempts to move away from just doing frontline work with children and families was to undertake specialist work with sex offenders. This was almost invariably with men; I was only once or twice asked to assess women who had been accused of perpetrating child sexual abuse. An example of assumptive questioning is, when the person being assessed has been found guilty of an offence, to phrase questions on the assumption that the offence took place, despite the man's denial.

I was privileged to be involved on a couple of occasions

with training put on by the late Ray Wyre, a leading figure in the assessment and treatment of sex offenders. On one of Ray's training programmes, he did a role play asking social workers to take turns in interviewing him. He took the role of a man with whom he had once worked, who had been caught by his wife in the bedroom of his naked teenage daughter. His story was that he had gone into the bedroom to remonstrate with her for having her music too loud. She had come out of a shower and was wrapped in a towel. She had laughed at him, he said, grabbed him to dance with her and in the process the towel had fallen off, and they had fallen on the bed. He denied abusing her.

Obviously, this was an implausible story, and participants in the training took turns in taking Ray through endless details of the incident to try to get him to change his story and to own up to his having abused her. Incidentally, sex offenders are past masters at putting blame for their abuse outside themselves, and often on the victim. This appeared to be a good instance of the man blaming the child.

We went around in circles for some time. When it came to my turn, I started immediately with an assumptive question. I assumed that there were other occasions in which he had been inappropriate with the child. My first question was, "Prior to this, when was the last time you saw your daughter naked?" Ray spoke of just such an occasion approximately a week before his wife saw him with her naked. He then ended the exercise saying that the man had been telling the truth about the occasion of his daughter asking to dance with him and the towel falling off. He had been abusing his daughter, though, which could account for her coquettish behaviour towards him on this occasion.

I have only once come across similar coquettish behaviour. I have referred earlier to the case of a fifteen-year-old who made allegations concerning her stepfather, but her mother was struggling as to whether to believe her or not. At the end of a difficult meeting I held with the three of them concerning this, in a cheeky and playful way, the girl grabbed at her stepfather's handkerchief poking out of his pocket.

I was taken aback, as it was so inappropriate on this occasion in my view: the meeting had been a painful and tense one, particularly for mother and daughter. It might seem innocent in normal, relaxed circumstances. It seemed to me to be rather provocative however, making a grab as she did so close to his groin area, straight after failing to convince her mother that he was sexually abusing her.

This seemed to me to be further evidence that abuse can tend to normalise inappropriate behaviour.

It is positive, though, that the development of understanding of the effects of child sexual abuse has meant that the problem no longer goes unrecognised. In the mid-1980s a foster parent who was on my caseload was arrested and imprisoned for this offence. I then reviewed the file carefully and saw that, very sadly, there was a pattern which had not been picked up, as there had been several changes of social worker. I found that virtually every child placed with him had subsequently displayed behaviour indicative of sexual abuse. What was particularly shocking was the fact that a child of about seven had made a disclosure, but a concluding comment of a manager upon investigation was that the child's allegation had "evidently been malicious". The manager cited the fact that the foster parent had taken the child to his GP about him masturbating to the extent of causing himself injury. It simply could not be believed that the foster parent would bring such a thing to the GP's attention if he were abusing the child.

I do believe that these days, it would never be concluded that a child of that age could make malicious allegations. Research indicates that some children can tell untruths of this nature, but instances are almost entirely confined to teenage children seeking to take revenge of some kind on an adult.

I failed the children placed in this foster placement after the child's disclosure. Unfortunately, with the pressure of work social workers are under, very often the files of cases of low concern are not scrutinised. I probably simply relied on the transfer summary provided by the previous worker, who also had not noticed a pattern developing.

These days, work with foster parents and adopters is carried out by specialist teams. In addition, local authorities – at least the ones I worked in – encourage the use of chronologies. These are a summary of concerns added regularly to the file as they happen, so that patterns can be picked up more easily.

Some colleagues asked me why I chose to work with sex offenders, saying they found the thought of doing so distasteful, to say the least. I responded that we all shared the aim of making children safer, and this work's aim was exactly to do that.

In later training, Ray Wyre's theme was that sex offenders are not monsters and do not walk around with any recognisable features. They do not have it written on their foreheads, so to speak, "I'm a paedophile". By this stage, the horrendous prevalence of men viewing child pornography online was becoming known. Ray was then arguing that such abusers are present in every community and cannot be locked away for ever. Working with perpetrators who come to light in an effort to address their offending behaviour is the least we can do to try to protect children.

* * *

Another attempt for me to do something different from front-line children and families work came about when the Mental Health Act of 1983 was enacted. This provided for social workers to be involved in the process of assessing if someone should be made subject to a Section ("be sectioned" as it was called colloquially). This could be under Section 2 for 28 days for assessment, or Section 3 for six months for treatment.

This is a truly drastic measure and I recall it being said that it was the only situation in which a person's liberty could be so drastically restricted without an order of a court.

The decision had to involve the approval of a doctor and a social worker. There was a requirement that the person should be interviewed "in a suitable manner". One of my colleagues said that on the first occasion she was called upon to assess someone in this way, the woman concerned was found to be standing on her head, stark naked, in a corner of her home. My colleague said she wondered how she could interview the woman "in a suitable manner" in such a situation!

Humorous situations can arise in social work, as in any profession, and can act as a relief in otherwise often sad and difficult work.

One of the more intense situations in which I was involved was when I was asked to see a man, Mr Stevens, who was living on his own. He had suffered a fire in his kitchen and half the floor was missing. Sadly, he was too unwell to do anything constructive about it. Mr Stevens spent most of his days striding at a fair pace around the town, covering large distances, appearing to be muttering to himself. I suggested to him that he needed an assessment in hospital. He offered to crucify me, an act he said he had already carried out on his psychiatrist. I declined the offer, and he strode away at his usual fast pace, no doubt to do another circuit of the town.

Paranoid schizophrenia had overtaken Mr Stevens. Many sufferers from this condition need compulsion to take necessary medication to control it, because a natural result of paranoia is to distrust those around who are trying to persuade the sufferer to do so.

Arranging a Section is quite a logistical exercise, as it is necessary for the doctor to be present to make his or her own assessment and to sign on the dotted line if there is agreement that the person should be sectioned. On occasions, police presence is deemed necessary and I certainly believed that it was necessary in this instance. Often, co-ordinating the visit with the presence of an ambulance was also thought needed in case travel to a hospital would result. An ambulance was not arranged on this occasion, as the hospital he would go to was not very distant.

I have related a time I suffered an assault despite the police being present, because they were otherwise occupied. I was distinctly disconcerted on this occasion when on my approach to Mr Stevens' door and his reacting in a highly agitated way, I discovered again that the police were nowhere in sight. Having been threatened with crucifixion, and the police being aware of that, I was rather aggrieved on realising this! I learned later that the police officers had decided to go around the back of the house in case the man sought to escape from a rear door.

Fortunately, the GP who was present was well known to his patient, and he approached the house with confidence once I had retreated, and I waited at the top of the driveway, keeping an eye on things. However, the GP was equally unable to persuade Mr Stevens to go into hospital, and he too had to retreat.

The police reappeared and they went into the home instead. I was amazed that within a few minutes, Mr Stevens appeared, apparently willing to be taken to hospital. In later discussion with the police officers, they said that the presence of a uniformed officer usually provokes one of two opposite reactions in such patients. It can have a calming and reassuring effect, as it did with Mr Stevens, or it can feed the paranoia further and have the effect of making the patient more agitated.

The GP and I signed the Section papers and I was asked to accompany the police to hospital with him. Again, I was disconcerted, as they asked me to sit next to Mr Stevens in the back of their car. They seemed confident that he would remain compliant, and in fact he did. I suppose I felt reassured that arranging a crucifixion in the back of a car might not be logistically easy!

Sadly, paranoid schizophrenia can have a deleterious effect for much of a sufferer's life. For many years subsequently I was to see Mr Stevens again striding around the streets of the town after his discharge from hospital.

Much has been written about Care in the Community replacing the previous practice of locking patients away in institutions for much of their lives. The need for good follow-up services in the community is obviously crucial for support to be an effective replacement for institutional care. My very limited involvement in the mental health field makes me a slightly informed person, very far from being an expert, but it seems positive to me that the emphasis is on keeping people in the community as long as they are not a danger to themselves or others.

Social work in the mental health field is yet another service that has become a specialised role, and no longer the remit of a social worker experienced in working in other fields like me. I think that that can only be right. For my part, though, I did find the work interesting and a break from my normal role.

Talking of the previous practice of long-term incarceration in institutions, I will always remember visiting the museum at the mental health hospital where I did my training. Part of the training was a placement there for a week, and I learned such a lot there. Looking at the past records in the museum, it was striking to read of the number of patients whose admission ended some years later in death. The only alternative entries were all "transferred", presumably to another institution, never "discharged". The development of drugs has enabled discharge into the community to be favoured these days.

I was to revisit this hospital on a few occasions subsequently. It was in a lovely rural setting, with a number of large Victorian buildings around extensive, green grounds. For many patients, tending the gardens was therapeutic.

One of my visits there was preceded by another rather tricky Section I was to carry out. This involved Mrs Green, a widow in her sixties living on her own. The referral to Social Services was from a builder who had been asked by Mrs Green to provide a quote for work on her bathroom. On visiting, he found the house in a very dirty and neglected state. The bathroom ceiling had fallen in following a water leak and the debris had blocked the toilet. Mrs Green was using a bucket in the garden.

I visited and found her to be a woman who was highly intelligent: apparently, she had been fluent in five or six languages and had acted as an interpreter in the European Community, as it was then. Mrs Green showed every indication of not having washed or bathed for some time – understandably, given the state of her home. She always applied makeup, though, and it seemed to be plastered on her face, giving her a severe look.

Although on the whole she seemed to be in touch with reality, her conversation turned quite frequently to lorries passing her property, headed for a business at the end of the road, and when she talked of these her voice became loud and agitated. Mrs Green was expressing paranoid ideas about the business seeking to ruin her life.

I felt that she needed assessment, given her level of agitation and the state of her home. I did not involve the police, as it seemed unnecessary, but instead arranged a GP and an ambulance, as she would need to be transported to the rural hospital some miles away if she were to be sectioned.

The GP readily agreed with me that Mrs Green needed a mental health assessment, but she was adamant that she would not go to hospital voluntarily. Her resistance became ever more strident and I was distressed when the ambulance crew wheeled her away, screaming. They were experienced, though, and both gentle and firm, holding her down in the wheelchair with a blanket.

A couple of days later I felt I should visit her, but I was rather dreading the reception I would get from her. Surely, after what I had put her through, I could expect nothing but hostility. My fears were unfounded. In fact, quite the opposite. Mrs Green was shrill and vocal, but only in praise for doing what I had done, declaring that this was just like a wonderful holiday! Clearly, the tranquillity and beauty of the setting had helped, in addition to medication, in calming her jangled nerves.

I had an interesting episode by way of a sequel to this. Mrs Green asked me to be present at her home when a builder she had arranged to give her a quote for repairs was due to visit. I was able to do so, letting us in with a key. Incidentally, we had arranged a cleaning party and a small army of Home Helps had blitzed the place, clearing the sink of old food and a dead rat, as well as having a general clean-up. Several black sacks had been filled and conveyed to the tip.

On exiting the property with the builder, we got chatting whilst looking over a fence opposite the property, as he was telling me that the couple of horses grazing there belonged to him. It was a gravel road we were on. Suddenly the tranquil scene was shattered by two police cars with flashing lights approaching at speed. They skilfully scrunched to a halt in a V shape, pinning us to the fence, and police officers spilled out. Fortunately, this being England, they were unarmed.

We were questioned over why we had been in Mrs Green's home. I had forgotten that I had arranged a Protection of Property through Social Services, and neighbours had been asked to inform the police if they saw any prowlers in or around the property. I apologised to them for wasting their time, but they told me not to worry, as they had enjoyed the exercise!

I will relate one more story on this theme. A referral had been received from neighbours of a woman, again I think in her sixties, whose milk deliveries were piling up uncollected and who was not responding to knocks on her door. I could do little other than try knocking on the door myself, without success.

We had no idea if she was alive and, if she was alive, whether she was simply medically ill or mentally unwell. I set up a Section, having obtained a warrant from a judge to enforce entry if needed: there was provision for such in the Mental Health Act for just such a situation as this.

This time, we had the works: the GP, of course, the police, as they had the authority and means of breaking into the property if needed, and an ambulance. It all felt highly dramatic. Again, there was no response to knocks or shouts at the door. The police were ready to break down the door, but one officer asked his colleagues to hold on a minute, and he put his foot on the bottom of the door. He explained that trying to rock the door could indicate if the Yale lock in the middle was the only means by which it was secured. In fact, at the slightest pressure of his foot, the door clicked open as the latch of the lock was barely making contact with the keep!

A few of us piled in, to find the woman serenely sitting on her settee, showing no real signs of alarm at the entry of several burly men – well, not terribly burly in my case, but it was certainly potentially highly alarming for the poor woman. I spoke to her for only a minute or two, saying that neighbours had been concerned about her not looking after herself, and suggesting that she needed to be assessed in hospital. Her response was, "Oh, all right then!"

She went off in the ambulance without further ado. After all the build-up, complex arrangements and drama, she was admitted as a voluntary patient.

I have sometimes wondered if I had sufficient expertise to carry out this role. My lack of specialism may have limited my ability to act appropriately and I am conscious that I never declined to support a Section on someone I was called on to assess for this.. The social worker's role was to give a non-medical oversight and to consider the person's general social circumstances.

Having said that, I equally cannot think of a case when I thought I had done the wrong thing. As the Act required, I took account of the views of the person's nearest relative, where possible. I think the closest I came to really wondering if a Section was justified was in the case of Mrs Green. Other than when the subject of passing trucks came up, her speech and ability to be in touch with reality were of no real concern. Her living circumstances were dire, but she had sought the help of the builder who had referred her in the first place.

My worries were considerably eased once I had visited

her in hospital. Deprivation of her liberty to the point of having her carted off tied down in a wheelchair was a drastic measure. There can be no doubt that she benefited from it though, and happily, that she appreciated the outcome.

A decision to support a Section is easier to decide upon when the person concerned is found naked upside down in a corner of a room, or when you are offered crucifixion. Sadly, deprivation of someone's liberty is necessary to get them the help they need. The decision is more difficult when the borderline must be drawn between eccentric behaviour and significant mental illness. The requirement of the Act to be assured that the person poses a risk to himself or others for a Section to be justified was an important component in placing a limitation on making such drastic decisions.

Chapter 8

Any other alternatives?

One further phase I experienced away from the front line was my venture into a local Family Centre in the mid-1990s. Here there was an excellent team with a range of skills working in the areas of assessment of families to inform case conferences and the courts. Also, work was carried out with families and individuals who were struggling with various difficulties and/or with abuse. The presence of an excellent team did not prevent the local authority from closing it a few years after my arrival. With the closure of this facility, as well as the residential unit shortly after my joining them, I must deny that my arrival in any way caused their closures. At least, I hope it didn't!

It was whilst in this setting that I undertook the training in, and work with, sex offenders. Being away from the unpredictabilities of front-line work also enabled me to begin a part-time Masters course in Child Protection with Kingston University. The manner in which the closure of the centre was handled by the local authority gave me wonderful material in the Managing Change module of the course, and my scathing analysis of the way in which it was carried out gained me a distinction.

The problem, as the local authority saw it, was that the centre had become too focused on assessment of high-risk cases and not on preventive work. The focus of a family centre should rather be support to young and inexperienced parents to prevent family breakdowns and crises.

The local authority planned an alternative for managing the child protection assessments that we had been carrying out by creating a centralised team within the county, about twenty miles from our current location. The slimmed-down staff group was to carry out such assessments as individuals working alongside the family's social worker, rather than as an independent team.

Such closures inevitably give rise to anxieties, sadness, and anger for the staff. I felt at risk of again ending up back in front-line work. Unqualified staff felt they had developed an expertise in assessments and that preventive work suggested they would become "bottle washers", in the words of one of them. Obviously, preventive work is both commendable and important, but this was the measure of the anger generated by the uncertainties.

I was able in my essay to use the literature available regarding the best ways of managing change in organisations to point out poor communication, prolonged uncertainty and an inability of the managers conducting the changes to convince staff that the changes would mean an improvement in services.

In working in the centre, I found my days much more predictable than when working in a front-line office. Not having responsibility for cases meant that there were no sudden callouts to investigate allegations or deal with crises. This was welcome, of course, but I actually found myself at times having a conscience over having such predictable hours and a lack of pressure when my front-line colleagues were still facing these difficulties.

Another noticeable difference was the relative absence of hostility. Being the allocated social worker to a family meant you were always in the firing line. I subsequently took the role of Children's Guardian in many cases after I became an Independent Social Worker – more of that later – and one feature of that role I found was listening to families who were angry at their social workers. Most often, it was anger and frustration with the local authority in general, but so much of that is focused on the social worker, who is after all the face of the local authority for the family.

I do not want to convey a sense that all social workers are seen that way. Even in the midst of the hostility that can surround court proceedings concerning children, many parents can make positive comments about social workers, although several of those are in making negative comparisons with their preferred social worker.

Of course, carrying out assessments can bring hostility when negative conclusions are reached. However, you can move on from this as you move on to the next case, leaving the allocated social worker again to "carry the can" forward. They are the ones who will continue to take the matter further in the courts, or to maintain monitoring home visits. Our assessments held few risks for staff (apart from that axe brought to an interview!) as they were carried out in the centre and therefore with several colleagues close by in the building.

Predictable engagements also enabled me to join a team carrying out groupwork with sex offenders, run a few miles away by another agency. It was great to be carrying out groupwork for the first time in my career, rather than just depending on my academic introduction to this form of social work way back in the past, at university in South Africa. It felt like a different skill to develop and it was interesting to be learning from colleagues working alongside me.

I found that the most powerful part of the course was a day-long session with a theatre group. Professional actors performed role plays in front of the men, inviting them to comment on what they saw. The men were readily able to point out the false justifications the actors were portraying in excusing the abuse.

Courses working with sex offenders in prison have of late come under attack, as a lack of analysis of the outcomes failed to spot that they had little or no effect and in fact, at times seemed to have the effect of making the participants more knowledgeable and more likely to reoffend.

Oh dear, here is another case of something being closed shortly after I joined! The agency decided that working with adult sex offenders did not accord with their overall aim of working with children, and the focus changed to the assessment of, and work with, adolescents accused of sexual abuse of children. The groupwork I was involved in therefore shut down. The programme did not last long enough, nor have a high enough intake, for the outcomes to be analysed. I can only hope that intensive work over several weeks had a positive effect on the men. Anecdotally, though, I hang on to one man's analysis of the effects on him. With great honesty he stated that he could not guarantee that he would not reoffend, given his attraction to adolescent males. However, he added, after the course he would not be able to convince himself that they wanted or enjoyed it.

We certainly focused much of the work on what was termed "distorted thinking". As I have mentioned before, men can be past masters at putting the blame outside themselves, and any view they entertained that the abuse was not serious, would not have potential long-term consequences, or in fact was sought by the victim, were strongly challenged by us in the groupwork. Such thinking as "She dressed in a way that was asking for it", "He gave me the come-on", "She looked older than she was/ lied about her age", "It just happened – I didn't plan it" can be commonplace among sex offenders. Sexual abuse of children does not just happen. The offender must have an orientation towards such behaviour. He or she then has to go through various stages to break down their own reticence to commit such an act, to overcome the child's resistance – hence the need to groom the child – and to evade the protective factors surrounding the child. If our work saved one child or adolescent from sexual abuse, then it was worth it.

I managed, for the first time, to make my next move in my career without an intervening stage of returning to front-line work. Well, sort of. I applied for, and gained, a post in a neighbouring authority based in a hospital. As it turned out, though, it became rather like front-line work, but based in a different setting. It felt different, though, and my role did involve contact with the children's ward and with midwives that I would not have had if I had been just part of a fieldwork team. The contact with the midwives also provided a sample for my Masters thesis focused on the impact of child protection matters in their work.

The idea of having a children and families social worker based in the hospital was a good one: the post had existed for a few years before I arrived. The hospital had a wide catchment area that covered three different district teams in Social Services. The cost of my salary was apparently shared by these three districts, but I was managed from the team local to the hospital.

By the time I arrived, I learned later, all three districts had had new managers appointed and it was only after some research that they learned that they were sharing the costs of maintaining my presence at the hospital. A further problem was that I became well known in the team within which I was managed, I was less well known in the team a bit down the motorway from me, and I was completely unknown by the team further down the motorway. The result was that I was contacted on matters connected to the hospital by members of my closest team, less frequently by the team further away and never by the furthest team.

I naturally made attempts to address this situation. A problem was that very many urgent referrals, as often happens with hospital work, came through agencies such as the police, who have very regular contact with the duty teams in Social Services. (Duty teams are the social work teams that deal with referrals when they first come in). Many also came outside normal office hours. The system therefore favoured these situations being taken forward in the normal way by the teams concerned without a thought that there was a social worker in the hospital available to do so.

Guess what? My placement in hospital lasted only a few years before I found myself again in a social work front line team. It felt as if there was an inevitable magnetic force running through my career drawing me towards this sort of placement. It came about mainly because of a lack of space for me at the hospital, but also a recognition that systems had moved forward to the point where it no longer made sense to have a children and families social worker permanently at the hospital.

Whilst I was at the hospital, I shared accommodation with a team of adult social workers. By this stage the experiment with social workers working with all age groups, outlined in a previous chapter, had long since been abandoned and in fact had got to the stage where many Social Services Departments had completely separate structures and management systems for work with children and families and with adults.

I gained great respect for my colleagues in the adult team. The pressure in a large hospital is unrelenting, with an urgency to prevent bed blocking.

Even during my fairly short time in the hospital I witnessed a great deal of expansion. This was most acutely felt, I think, by staff in regard to the car park, with ever greater restrictions being placed on staff being allowed to bring their car to work.

Inevitably, expansion of the hospital meant expansion of the adult team, coupled with pressure on them to relinquish their space in the hospital. It was agreed among managers that the children and families post at the hospital should be ended. It had become less relevant as systems for referral had moved forward, as I have described. I learned that soon after I left, the adult team was moved into a prefabricated building in the hospital grounds.

During my time at the hospital, I would often hold onto cases I dealt with from the local area long after the hospital involvement had ended. That is why I referred to this work being at least partly the same as being in front-line social work.

A great deal of social work can be described as unhappy, in one way or another. After all, social workers become involved in families when things are going wrong. In the hospital I became involved in some particularly sad situations. One such involved sudden infant death investigations, often referred to as cot death. Frequently, there is no definable medical causation found and the system has to treat all such cases as ostensibly suspicious. It seems particularly pernicious to be interviewing parents still reeling from the discovery of their dead infant in a manner that clearly aims to see if they had caused the death. It was fortunate that the medical staff I worked alongside, and the police officers, were also very aware of the sensitive way such interviews need to be conducted. Also, none of these investigations I had to undertake found anything suspicious.

One lasting memory I have of my early days in the hospital was having a case referred to me of what was termed 'shaken baby syndrome'. The poor little lad concerned had been rushed off to a London specialist hospital in a touch-and-go attempt to save his life. This was successful, but involved creating a shunt in his head to relieve his brain of the pressure of internal bleeding. He was returned to our hospital once he was well enough, and I decided to go to the ward to meet him for the first time. Oh dear, what a sight greeted me. His head was badly distorted, a large scar ran across his scalp and he had a severe squint. I talked to him quietly and was rewarded by a huge smile! He was a real fighter. I had other cases of this syndrome, but none as serious, I am pleased to say.

Matters where medical evidence clashes with strong denial and against a general pattern in a family can be particularly difficult. Medical opinion can be convincingly put forward that the evidence points to abuse, either through shaking or trauma to the body. Retinal bleeding and bleeding to the brain are strong indicators as are, obviously, broken bones. Nevertheless, parents could be very convincing too in showing incredulity and denying any knowledge of how this could have come about.

Interestingly, this was another type of case that could get me involved with middle class families if there was an absence of indicators of concern, such as poverty, drug and alcohol abuse, unstable backgrounds, mental health problems, unemployment, and multiple relationships.

Systems are in place to try to address these tricky decisions for social workers, chiefly case conferences and ultimately, of course, the courts. Case conferences are meetings between different agencies aimed at deciding whether the child or children need to be subject to a Child Protection Plan. The conference then draws up a plan as to how their welfare can be monitored, and by which agencies. Courts are involved where the concerns are significant enough to consider whether stronger action is needed.

* * *

During my time at the hospital I became involved in a local multi-agency forum seeking to co-ordinate domestic violence services in the area. My career, as with any children and families social worker, has had a huge amount of involvement with this ubiquitous problem. It is getting a great deal of press coverage during the Covid 19 lockdown as I write, with families thrown together and given limited opportunity to get out of the home to relieve tensions.

There are many reasons why victims of domestic abuse remain in such relationships. Abusive partners can be very persuasive in saying they will mend their ways. There can be financial dependence, low self-esteem, fear of the abuse and yet fear of the consequences of trying to leave, concern about the effect on the children of ending the relationship, amongst many others.

One particularly tricky case which illustrates the dilemmas some women face was that of Miss Baker. I cannot recall how I became involved initially, as she did not present at the hospital with injuries. However, she came to attention because she had a two-year-old and a baby by her partner, Charles, and their welfare was being threatened by the level of abuse in the relationship.

The children were made subject to a Child Protection Plan, which required Miss Baker to protect them through ending the relationship with Charles. She seemed keen to do so. However I was, in the end, supporting her through four moves of home before this was ensured. The police provided her with a plan for protection within the family home, but this failed to keep Charles away. He even managed to find her when she moved to a refuge many miles away. She agreed to move to another refuge at the other end of the county, but Charles was seen outside this location after a time. By this time, I was having concerns that Miss Baker was not being honest with us.

Most often, by this stage, court action would be taken to protect the children. Was she disclosing their whereabouts to Charles? Women can often feel torn about depriving the children of contact with their father. Many times I have heard women say that they had grown up without a father and they desperately wanted to avoid that for their children.

I cannot recall what persuaded me in the end to argue with managers that we should give Miss Baker one further final chance to prove herself able to protect the children. In fact, they had not been further harmed, other than having to live in new places so often. However, remaining with their mother throughout, at that age, will have largely mitigated the effects of being moved around.

Miss Baker agreed to move to another county. I recall speaking to her on the telephone a couple of days after she moved and being told that she was determined to ensure the children remained in her care, but it was a struggle. She tried to go into the town on the day after she arrived and was refused entry onto the bus with her double buggy, as there was insufficient room. She felt that this was an inauspicious start to life as a single parent in strange surroundings so far away from her mother's support, and it did not help with maintaining her morale and determination. I really felt for her, knowing how much she had struggled with having to move so far away.

Her new local authority will know if the move was successful in the longer run or not. My last visit was to attend a transfer case conference and to wish Miss Baker all the best for the future. By then she was showing definite signs of settling finally.

The press – and indeed many parents I have dealt with – are very quick to accuse social workers of itching to take children into care. Of course, when children remain with parents and things go terribly wrong, the press is equally vociferous in their condemnation for not protecting them. The fact is that a huge amount of effort goes into keeping children with their parents or, if that is not possible, for the children to be cared for by wider family.

In any case when social workers do decide to seek removal of the children, lengthy court proceedings follow to ensure that the right decision has been made. I can particularly attest to that. What a contrast between the situation in which my decision-making was scrutinised only by a single Children's Commissioner in South Africa, with the parents assisted by him or her but not by a solicitor, and what now pertains in England.

Proceedings in South Africa seldom took more than an hour or two. When I first arrived in England the situation was a little different, in that parents were always (and still are) assisted through Legal Aid to be represented, but still proceedings could last only two or three hours. That is what made the case of Cindy that I outlined earlier so different, with the proceedings lasting four or five days.

These days final hearings lasting a week or two are not so uncommon. No one can accurately predict the future, but every effort is made to try to make decisions based on the best possible prediction for the child's future welfare.

Chapter 9

Independence

The next, and final, step in my career was to become an Independent Social Worker in 2006. I had been working in government or local authority departments for over thirty years and it again felt like there was a need for change to keep myself motivated and to continue to broaden my horizons.

So much of my work had involved court work and I was by now as comfortable with writing reports for the court, attending court, instructing solicitors, and giving evidence as I could be. Giving evidence and facing cross-examination can never be a comfortable experience, but familiarity and practice naturally make things easier. By the end, I was able to be sworn in without referring to the card given to me by the clerk with the wording on. I swore on the bible: "I swear by Almighty God that the evidence I shall give shall be the truth, the whole truth and nothing but the truth." Most people these days "affirm", rather than swearing on the bible.

Since the 1980s, in addition to the social worker, children involved in local authority proceedings have had a guardian *ad litem*, nowadays called a Children's Guardian, and a solicitor to represent them. Decisions about children that led to subsequent abuse, and even death, led legislators to believe that children needed a voice in proceedings concerning their future.

It is important for the Children's Guardian to be independent of the local authority for obvious reasons: he or she is representing the child and could well be opposing the local authority's position. The service was initially provided by Independent Social Workers (ISWs), experienced workers who were self-employed. In the 1990s the service was subsumed into the Children and Family Courts Advice and Support Service, CAFCASS. Although CAFCASS initially wanted Children's Guardians to become employees of the agency, resistance by the independent workers led to an acceptance that CAFCASS would contract some of the cases to ISWs.

At the time I was considering becoming an ISW, I believe CAFCASS had accepted that they could not have all the work of Children's Guardians, as well as the other court services they were providing, undertaken by their employed staff – there was simply too much work to go around. They were therefore on occasion advertising for ISWs who were willing to take on such contracts to come onto their books.

Having worked for so long in local authorities, I was fortunate to be in a secure enough financial position to make the leap into being self-employed, with the financial uncertainty that results. However, the decision was considerably eased by CAFCASS accepting me as a suitable candidate and my resignation from my final position in a children and families social work team followed.

Acting as Children's Guardian in cases for CAFCASS for a few years initially made local solicitors aware that I was now independent, and slowly requests came in for me to provide an independent assessment. If I agreed, and I had no previous knowledge of, or connection to, the case, they would ask the court to agree. In such cases, although instructed by a solicitor, or all the solicitors involved jointly, one is an expert witness to assist the court: neutral, therefore, rather than acting for any one of the parties.

Being a Children's Guardian is exacting, because it is your job to interview all relevant family members and review the evidence of all the parties including the social worker. Your report is then the final submission. This spells out the views of the child or children and gives your own arguments about whether you support the local authority's plans or not. If the child is too young to give you their views, you do the best you can to act in their best interests.

It is exacting because the Children's Guardian's view carries a lot of weight. I have experienced only a handful of cases where my recommendation has not been accepted by the court. Of course, I could say that is because I was so good at my work! However, sadly I cannot do so with any honesty, as this is the experience of all Children's Guardians as far as I know. The fact is that, in most cases, the outcome is fairly obvious and uncontroversial as it is plainly the best outcome that could be considered to be in the child's best interests.

Very often, therefore, by the stage of the final hearing the parents concede to, or at least do not oppose, the plans put forward. It is of considerable advantage that the parents are automatically represented through Legal Aid, and their solicitor can be very useful in advising the parents whether opposing the plans has any likelihood of succeeding or not.

Finally, it is exacting because the Children's Guardian's length of experience can put one into a position almost like an expert and cross-examination can be difficult. No matter how experienced one is, I would guess that no one really wants to go through being repeatedly questioned about why one is opposing arguments that are being put forward. Sometimes I felt confident of my arguments, but cases can be complex and nuanced and, in such cases, defending my position could be problematic.

In addition, putting forward arguments that must be painful for parents to listen to, was always emotionally draining. Of course, the focus is the children, but it must be terribly difficult to be a parent sitting listening to evidence against the children being returned to their care. Most difficult is when the arguments are supporting adoption, meaning a complete severance of the parents' relationship with the children.

Cross-examination in the Family Courts is, in the vast majority of cases, done sympathetically and not in an attacking way and certainly not in a personally confrontational manner. Things are now very different compared to the time in South Africa when I faced a solicitor who was experienced only in criminal courts and sneered at me about my "vast" two-and-a-half years' experience!

Nevertheless, it was when I was on my way to court one day, thinking that I was not really looking forward to facing cross-examination, that I began to think about retirement. It struck me that I was past normal retirement age and had done more than forty years of social work, and I wondered why I was still putting myself through experiences that can be emotionally draining. That made the decision to retire an easy one. I took no further work on and spent the next few months finishing off my existing cases.

* * *

One thing I noticed about the Children's Guardian role is how much less hostility I encountered. Having come from a role in which I was the social worker seeking to remove the children and therefore having a very difficult relationship with the parents, I felt uncomfortable, but also rather relieved, at listening to parents complaining about their social worker rather than about me. Not fair, but I had had very many years of being on the other end of it.

I was quite amazed by this. Even after I had given

evidence against them, I did not encounter hostility from parents. On only one occasion that I can remember did I receive a look that could kill. That case was one of the most nuanced I encountered, when I was involved with a mother for the second time.

The first set of proceedings had been relatively straightforward, or at least as straightforward as any case involving children can be. The mother had really messed up the life of her six-year-old son, Peter, through her tendency to lie, her unstable lifestyle and her poor parenting skills. There had been extensive involvement of a local authority even before she suddenly left that area without letting her social worker know. They were found when Peter was enrolled in a new school, and this local authority started court proceedings to determine his future. Peter remained in his mother's care pending the outcome.

During an interview I was having with his mother he started throwing things around in temper and she gave him a resounding smack across the leg in my presence. The court was amazed that she would do this in front of his Children's Guardian, and at the next hearing, it decided that Peter should be moved into foster care. The final hearing ended with him remaining in long-term foster care.

It was subsequent proceedings that arose when his mother became pregnant again that were particularly difficult. Peter had been saying that he was frightened of a male friend of his mother's. She swore in her statement to court that this man was not the baby's father.

She went into a parent and baby foster placement with her daughter and really did remarkably well with her during the months that it took to reach a final hearing.

Mother and baby foster placements are where remarkable foster carers agree to have a parent or parents live in with them, together with their baby, to support them and, in need, teach them parenting skills. This mother was different from the average such placement, as she was older and familiar with looking after a baby: the placement was mainly to monitor her general lifestyle and coping abilities.

I saw Peter again during these proceedings, as I observed a contact he had with his mother and his baby half-sister. He was doing well in foster care and having monthly supervised contact with his mother. Shortly before the baby's final hearing, the local authority investigated the mother's social media account and gave evidence that the man she had denied was the father was in fact the father.

After further denial, she retracted her original statement and said she was sorry for lying. She explained that she had been frightened that revealing the paternity would lead the court almost inevitably to remove the baby from her care. She promised that she was not in a relationship with this man, but only visited him on occasions, and she would stay the night after drinking alcohol with him as a friend.

I faced lengthy cross-examination, not only by the solicitors but also by the judge, because despite the mother doing well with her daughter I felt that, all things being taken into account, she could not be trusted enough to keep the baby safe once she left the parent and baby foster placement. There was just too much of a history, I argued, of her lying, leading an unstable lifestyle and not managing when the child's behaviour became challenging.

The local authority was with me in this, but what made things even more difficult was the fact that the mother had had the court's permission to have an Independent Social Worker provide an expert opinion, and the ISW had recommended that the baby remain with the mother. What a difficult one for the judge!

In the end, the judge supported the local authority's position. The baby went for adoption and I really do hope she did better than she would have done in such an unreliable mother's care. As always, I will never know.

* * *

Carrying out independent assessments involves quite a bit of travel. My motorbike, in use since my hospital days, did a few thousand miles each year taking me to visits and courts. ISWs are scattered and one can be asked to do assessments quite a long way away. Distance is limited, at least in part, by the requirements of the Legal Aid Agency in their efforts to keep costs down.

It all takes a fair amount of planning and effort to ensure that visits can be made on the way to and/or from the more distant clients to provide for sharing of costs between the cases, thus minimising the total cost to each case. But it is tiring. I found myself becoming familiar with bed and breakfasts, guesthouses and hotels in various locations. I bore the cost of these, simply because it made life simpler for me and obviated long journeys home late at night.

A technique I learned for assessments that I particularly enjoyed using, and did so on every occasion I could, is called Story Stem Assessment (SSA). I attended a course at the Anna Freud Centre in London to become accredited in using this. (Perhaps it was portentous that it was her name that I recognised from the list of psychologists that the lawyer confronted me with in South Africa!) I like working with figures; my early career in banking, and subsequent voluntary work as treasurer for churches and charities attest to that.

SSA is used for children aged about four to eight years of age. They need to be reasonably articulate – hence the minimum of four – and not have a tendency to manipulate responses to suit what they think the interviewer wants to hear (children may do this after the age of about eight). SSA involves using toy figures and giving the child a beginning of a story and asking the child to finish it. There are thirteen stories, and each has a slightly tricky dilemma for the child to resolve.

The sessions are video recorded so that responses can be analysed later and given a score. The Anna Freud Centre had done studies with two groups – children from stable backgrounds, and adopted children who had had disrupted early experiences and relationships. You can then check the scores of the child you have worked with against these standardised scores. This gave an indication of aspects of the child's attachment patterns, and whether they tended toward the stable group's scores or the disrupted group's scores.

As part of the accreditation process, I had to carry out the exercise with a willing guinea pig, a friend's child. He gave sensible, calm endings to his stories and, true to expectations given his stable family upbringing, landed scores that were well within the Anna Freud Centre's stable background figures in all areas.

As I say, I loved doing this. I was fascinated by the way the children elaborated on the stories. I experienced a good spread of children, from those who were shy, anxious and rather monosyllabic in their responses, needing some prompting, to those who enthusiastically launched into long and elaborate stories, requiring intervention to get them to finish the story. It may be unsurprising that some boys tended to like blood and destruction in their stories! These children usually landed up with scores well within the disrupted group scores.

I used this tool in a case I dealt with in which a father was challenging the mother's decisions over seven-year-old Alice and five-year-old Brenda having contact with him. He did this by applying for them to be moved into his care. There had been involvement of the local authority over allegations of the mother hitting Brenda and although Child Protection Plans had followed, the local authority had not themselves taken court proceedings.

The arguments on the side of each parent were quite well balanced. One of the criteria the law requires courts to consider in decisions about children is the likely effect on them of change. Given that the children had been in their mother's care all their lives, a decision to move them to their father's care would be difficult to argue for.

The SSA results for both Alice and Brenda put them well in the category of the unstable cohort produced by the Anna Freud Centre. I would not have expected this: after all, they had been consistently in their mother's care. It was an indication, though, how much disruption had been caused to them by the breakup of the parents' relationship, the mother's inability to manage them calmly, and reluctance to work with their father.

Research indicates that children can get over parents separating, but ongoing disputes between the parents have serious adverse effects on them. Alice and Brenda were a case in point, I felt.

The Anna Freud Centre emphasises that SSA is not an assessment in itself, but a tool to inform a wider assessment. In this case, I felt that the SSA results tipped the balance in favour of a move to their father, who seemed more able to be reasonable in his views about his ex-wife than she was regarding him.

The judge commented during my evidence in court that the SSA was "a bit technical". I agreed, but said that attachment is important. Secure attachment to a stable adult figure in a child's early years is important in allowing the child to reach her potential. Alice and

Brenda scored highly in the area of insecure attachment.

The court decided on the children being moved to their father, with regular contact with their mother. Again, I sincerely hope that my intervention had, on balance, a positive effect on them. As I have said before, no one can predict the future accurately and all social workers, and judges, can do is to do the best they can in doing so.

I continued as a Children's Guardian and doing independent work, but also branched out further in my work for CAFCASS towards the end of my career in one of the most difficult areas of work, to my mind – Private Law. When it is the local authority bringing proceedings to the court, it is termed Public Law. When parents start proceedings over where children should live and how contact can be maintained, it is known as Private Law.

Some ISWs resist working in Private Law, as it can be the most vexed area to work in. I believe there can be few arenas in which there can be more bitterness and hostility than when divorcing couples are in dispute over possessions and children.

I am thankful that few official complaints have been made against me in my career, but I believe that in the few years I undertook Private Law work towards the end I had more complaints raised against me than in all the rest of my career combined. A colleague mentioned to me that a complaint was raised against her in the very first Private Law case she undertook, and she believed that in CAFCASS it almost comes with the territory.

It has probably come across in my musings that I have experienced a great deal of sadness at various times during my time as a social worker. I think I can honestly say that nothing has caused as much sadness as parents who tear their children's lives apart through a stubborn refusal to see the other's point of view, or who pursue litigation endlessly despite the negative effects on the children.

Chapter 10

Final reflections

Let me end my reflections on a happier note. I will go several years back in my career to talk about young Ben. Ben was three or four years old when I removed him from his mother's care. I cannot remember why this occurred, but the evidence against his mother must have been sufficient to justify Ben being placed for adoption.

I was lucky enough to carry the case through to the final outcome. I remember that a lovely couple was put forward as potential adopters for Ben, but it was not altogether straightforward, as the adoptive father was about twenty years older than his wife and of advancing years, shall I say. There was much debate about this, as it seemed a real possibility that Ben might experience bereavement before he attained his majority.

All other factors seemed right, however. The adoptive father could give five-year-old Ben (as he was by then) full-time care when he was not at school. Most likely, Ben would experience continued good care from his adoptive mother even if her husband should die whilst Ben was still dependent, but also they would still be well able to manage financially.

The match between Ben and these prospective adopters was in the end approved and in due course we attended court for the court to make the adoption order. It was all done in a quite informal way, as Ben would be present, and the judge was able to make it a happy experience.

I had been invited to attend their home for tea that afternoon by way of celebration. When I turned up, there was young Ben in dinner suit and black bowtie, ready to serve me from his "silver" tray with lovely cakes and tea. A truly happy memory for me. I am sure you had a good life, Ben, certainly better than the life you would have had if you had remained with unstable parents. After all, that has been the primary focus of my career: support children to stay with parents if at all possible, and if that really does not look good enough, seek the best possible alternative to help them achieve their potential.

My overall thoughts? I have no regrets about my choice of career. It has been hard at times. It has been emotionally draining at times. I have had sleepless nights on occasion. I have felt frustration with the bureaucracy of government and local authority work. It certainly takes a degree of resilience to manage changes brought in by management, particularly when you have been working in the field for years and feel that the changes are simply taking you back to where you started.

However, I believe that I have made a difference. For some children that has meant a lifelong change of circumstances. Throughout, I have believed that the actions I have carried out have been in the child's best interests, although on occasions the decisions on what action to take have been finely balanced. No one can accurately predict the future for children, and I have sought to analyse possible outcomes as carefully as possible to reach the best solution.

I have always been grateful for the checks and balances applied by the courts in deciding whether my analysis and conclusions are indeed the right ones for the child. I noted that this process is far more complicated in England than I experienced in South Africa, and during my career it has become more complicated. However frustrating the court process can be though, it is designed to ensure that social workers and local authorities do not have excessive powers of interference. In addition, the support of managers and colleagues in thinking things through has been invaluable.

Primarily, I have felt privileged during my career to have been able to get to know children who needed help, to do my best to understand their needs and wishes and to help them to achieve their true potential.

Printed in Great Britain
by Amazon